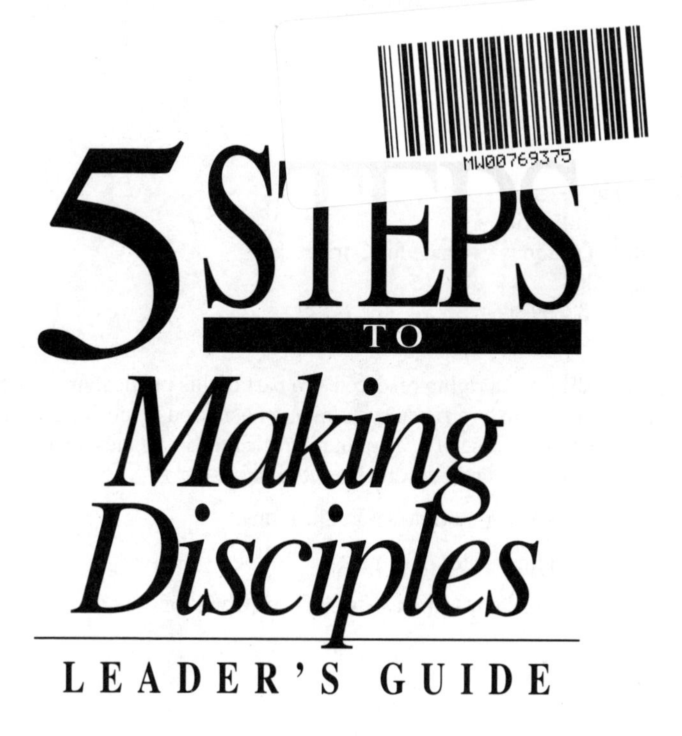

5 Steps to Making Disciples

LEADER'S GUIDE

Bill Bright

NewLife Publications
A MINISTRY OF CAMPUS CRUSADE FOR CHRIST

Five Steps to Making Disciples
Leader's Guide

Published by
New*Life* Publications
A ministry of Campus Crusade for Christ
P.O. Box 593684
Orlando, FL 32859-3684

Design and typesetting by Genesis Publications.

Printed in the United States of America.

Distributed in Canada by Campus Crusade for Christ of Canada, Surrey, B.C.

ISBN 1-56399-055-5

As a personal policy, Bill Bright has never accepted honorariums or royalties for his personal use. Any royalties from this book or the more than fifty books and booklets by Bill Bright are dedicated to the glory of God and designated to the various ministries of Campus Crusade for Christ/*New**Life2000***.

For more information, write:

Life Ministries—P.O. Box 40, Flemington Markets, N5W 2129, Australia
Campus Crusade for Christ of Canada—Box 300, Vancouver, B.C., V6C 2X3, Canada
Campus Crusade for Christ—Fairgate House, King's Road, Tyseley, Birmingham, B11 2AA, England
Campus Crusade for Christ—P.O. Box 8786, Auckland, New Zealand
Campus Crusade for Christ—Alexandra, P.O. Box 0205, Singapore, 9115, Singapore
Great Commission Movement of Nigeria—P.O. Box 500, Jos, Plateau State Nigeria, West Africa
Campus Crusade for Christ International—100 Sunport Lane, Orlando, FL 32809, USA

Contents

A Personal Word

Of all the great challenges you have heard of or participated in, which one brings the most joy and benefit? I have found that nothing compares with the privilege of introducing others to Christ, thereby helping to fulfill the Great Commission as given by our Lord in Matthew 20:18–20. That is my firm conviction, and my experience over the years has confirmed it.

Someone once asked, "In light of your long ministry for our Lord and the lessons you have learned since you started Campus Crusade for Christ in 1951, what would you do differently?"

This was a topic about which I had strong convictions, so I responded, "I would concentrate more on winning and training men and women of God (building disciples) whom He has already chosen and ordained to be His spokesmen to the world."

That is what Jesus emphasized in the Great Commission and what the apostle Paul instructed Timothy, his son in the faith, as recorded in 2 Timothy 2:2:

> The things you have heard me say in the presence of many witnesses entrust to reliable men who will also be qualified to teach others.

Although Campus Crusade's major thrust since its inception has been winning others to Christ, building them in their faith, training and discipling believers to become fruitful witnesses, then sending them out to help fulfill the Great Commission, my conviction about its importance has intensified. If I could change my past ministry, I would place a greater emphasis on building disciples who are committed to the fulfillment of the Great Commission. For those who respond to the call, I would seek to inspire, motivate, and train them to understand the greatness of God and His plan for men and women.

There is no question in my mind that the prayers and witness of godly, Spirit-filled men and women can reverse the tide of evil that is threatening to destroy all that we hold dear and sacred in our Judeo-Christian faith. The key to changing the world is spiritual multiplication—winning and training men and women who in turn win and train others who go on to win and train still others, spiritual generation after spiritual generation. (This principle is explained more fully in the next section.) That is the strategy the church used in the first centuries to reach the world with God's message. And it is the same strategy we are using to touch the lives of people all over the world today.

This principle is seen so clearly in the life of a Thai Christian whom I met some time ago. Charlie Wanagit was at that time the spiritual father of twelve generations of believers. Charlie, who had led more than 1,500 people to Christ in the past four years, introduced me to one of his disciples, who introduced me to one of his disciples, and so it went down a line of twelve men and women. The last disciple in the chain had been a Christian only six months and had already introduced twelve people to Christ!

But tragically, many Christians today are not true disciples of our Lord Jesus Christ. Instead, they are content to "play church" while living a materialistic and selfish lifestyle. Yet many others have demonstrated sacrificial love for God and for building His kingdom.

God is an all-powerful, loving, wise, and compassionate heavenly Father! Nothing is too hard for Him. He is looking for true disciples—men and women who are willing to put their lives on the line for Him, who will use their resources to win, build, train, and send others in order to help fulfill the Great Commission. I challenge you to be part of His plan to take the most joyful news ever announced of His love and forgiveness to every person on earth. God will richly bless you for your obedience, and you will experience the reality of our Lord's promise to reveal Himself to all who love and obey Him (John 14:21).

Only one life, 'twill soon be past;
only what's done for Christ will last.

The Principle of Spiritual Multiplication

Imagine for a moment that you are a great evangelist. The intense desire of your heart is to help fulfill the Great Commission (Matthew 28:18–20) that Christ gave us before He left this earth. You share the message of God's love and forgiveness through Jesus Christ wherever you go and 1,000 people each day come to Christ as a result of your ministry.

At that rate, how long do you think it would take you to reach the world for Christ? Assuming that the population did not grow, it would take approximately 15,000 years!

This is what I call spiritual addition. But God has given His children a miraculous strategy called spiritual multiplication through which we can reach the world in our generation. Spiritual multiplication is purposefully discipling new Christians so that they in turn will evangelize and disciple others, spiritual generation after spiritual generation.

Boonma Panthrasi, our director in Thailand, is an amazing example of spiritual multiplication. He and his wife, Chalong, received their training at our Great Commission Training Center in the Philippines in 1980. They returned to Thailand, and within six years he trained 700 individuals to share their faith in Christ and teach others to do the same. In turn, these disciples have trained 90,000 and are now involved in winning and discipling still others.

For example, Boonma trained Boonhiang, a new Christian, how to follow-up new believers. Boonhiang was so excited about his Lord that he would not go one day without talking to others about Jesus Christ. Soon, he became part of a "JESUS" film team, traveling with the group to show the "JESUS" film all over the area. Since he used the *Four Spiritual Laws* as a witnessing tool, he asked Boonma to make a flip chart with the words and diagrams so he could use it to speak to large groups. As soon as he received the flip chart, he carried it wherever he went.

As of today, Boonhiang has personally shared his faith in Christ with 200,000 people. And more than 20,000 have received Christ through this man's witness. At 74 years of age, Boonhiang is still active for his Lord and can count more than forty spiritual generations of Christians involved in evangelism and discipleship. As a result, the church he leads in his hometown has fourteen daughter churches. His witness is so vibrant that he receives many invitations to pioneer a work in another area or to debate with native religious radicals, including many Buddhists. In the long run, he wins his arguments, but does so with peace. He has introduced many of his listeners to Jesus Christ.

But Boonhiang's zeal for the Lord has also come with a price. He has suffered persecution for his faith, but God has always protected him. He has been stoned. He has been shot at by gangsters—but all their bullets missed. Thieves who tried to rob him were blinded. When Communists trapped him in the jungle, he boldly witnessed to them. Some of them received Christ, and after four days he was released unharmed. His example emphasizes the importance of training new believers how to witness effectively and boldly for our Lord and to persevere in following Him.

These believers know that it is not enough just to lead others to the Lord, and say, "Isn't it great?"—then leave them alone to grow spiritually by themselves. Rather, these spiritual multipliers win people and disciple them, training the new Christians to win and disciple others so they, in turn, will win and disciple still others. If we properly communicate the basic principles of our faith to new Christians, many will grow into spiritual multipliers.

I am often reminded of the personal motto of my beloved friend, Dawson Trotman, founder of the Navigators: "Born to reproduce." That describes New Testament Christianity. Boonhiang's ministry is a dramatic example of that concept of New Testament Christianity in our century.

You and I can be spiritual multipliers, too. If each of us would win just one person to Christ and train him to disciple others, who would in turn win and disciple others, we could reach the world for Christ in this generation!

I encourage you before this day is over to ask yourself, "Am I committed to influencing my world for Jesus Christ? If so, am I giving myself to spiritual multiplication or to spiritual addition?" If you have a desire to build spiritual qualities into the lives of others, ask God to lead you to several individuals through whom you can build a chain of multipliers. Then give to these brothers and sisters in Christ your vision for the Great Commission and the importance of spiritual multiplication. Watch how God will use you to reach people you could never touch through spiritual addition.

The lessons in this book were designed to help you teach other Christians how to reproduce spiritually. By the end of these five Steps, your students will be ready to begin their own multiplying ministries. As you lead your small group study, you will see your members get excited about leading their own group and showing individuals whom they have introduced to Christ how to do the same. In time, your group can multiply into many groups which will in turn produce even more groups. By studying and leading these five lessons, you will learn how to:

- Follow-up new and older Christians
- Motivate and encourage others to make disciples
- Help group members lead their own discipleship groups

Enjoy the excitement of seeing your disciples become disciplers, resulting in a dynamic ministry right in your community! I am confident that our Lord will multiply your ministry as you begin to train others.

How to Lead a Small Group Bible Study

Perhaps you feel less than confident about leading a small group Bible study. If God has led you to be a leader, He will give you the power and wisdom to accomplish the task. You do not need to be a theologian, Bible scholar, or great teacher to guide a group in studying this material. God uses ordinary people who have a heart for Him and who make themselves available to do His will.

Personal preparation is a vital first step to becoming a godly leader. To be an effective leader:

- You should have previously, by faith, received Jesus Christ as your Savior and Lord.
- You should know the reality of living moment by moment in the power of the Holy Spirit.
- You should have a heart for God and for His truths as revealed in His holy Word, the Bible.
- You should desire to help others learn these truths and be willing to devote time and effort to leading a group.

If you meet these simple requirements, you are ready to assemble your group.[1]

Assembling Your Study Group

The first and most important step is to pray for God's leading and blessing. Then invite Christian friends who have a basic knowledge of God's Word and the Christian life to attend your group. Select people you think will be interested in deepening

---

[1] I encourage you to read these two books: *The Secret* and *Witnessing Without Fear*. They contain the basic principles for living the victorious Christian life. Order from a Christian bookseller or from New*Life* Publications at (800) 235-7255.

their ministry. (Step 5, "Prepare to Lead a Discipleship Group," is a study on how to begin a small group Bible study. If you need more help in beginning a group of your own, you may want to look over this lesson.) Once you have a list of names, pray about each person's involvement, then visit each prospective group member personally.

Keep your group small to avoid losing a feeling of intimacy. With eight to twelve people, group members will feel freer to interact and to discuss the lesson material. You will also have more time to give your students individual attention as they begin to apply biblical truths in their lives.

Avoid pressuring anyone to join your group. At the same time, do not have a negative or apologetic attitude. The best way to promote interest and enthusiasm is to be interested and enthusiastic yourself. As you pray and wait on God, He will lead you to those He has chosen for your study.

Once you have identified interested participants, select a meeting place and time for your Bible study that is convenient for those who will attend. If several days lapse between your initial contact and the first study session, remind group members with a note or phone call.

Be sure to order a Study Guide (available from your favorite Christian bookseller or New*Life* Publications) for each member of your group.

Guidelines for Leading

The Leader's Guide is carefully designed to help you guide your students' discovery of spiritual principles and to show how these truths can be applied to their lives. Your main activity will be studying the Scriptures, and any discussion should follow the study outline in the lesson plan.

The following guidelines will help you lead the sessions:

- Bring extra Bibles and pencils for students to use during the study time.

- Create an informal atmosphere so you and your group can get acquainted. Address each person by name, and introduce new members before the discussion begins.
- Keep your Bible open at all times. The lesson material uses the *New International Version*.
- Be yourself. Depend on the Holy Spirit to work through the person you are, not through an artificial "spiritual leader" image that you would like to project.
- Don't be bound to your notes. Maintain eye contact with your group.
- Center the discussion around your students. A group leader is a discussion guide, not a lecturer. You should be prepared to suggest ideas, give background material, and ask questions to keep the conversation lively and relevant, but do not dominate the discussion. Instead, draw out comments from your students. The informal nature of a small group study is ideal for helping students learn from each other as well as from the things you say. (See the following section on how to encourage participation.)
- If a student is saying something pertinent, refrain from inserting your own thoughts. When he finishes, clarify and summarize if necessary.
- Avoid controversial theological teachings that could cause confusion among group members.
- Get involved in the lives of your group members. Communicating the basic truths of the Christian life is more than passing on information; it is sharing life experiences. Help members put into practice the truths you are teaching. The way you model and mentor through your personal example will have a far greater impact on your group than any of the words you say in a meeting.
- Be punctual about beginning and closing the session.

Keep in mind that each group has its own personality—some groups are active, others more subdued. Adapt your leadership style to fit your group. Remember, your most important quality as a leader is to be open to the Holy Spirit's guidance as you help your students explore and apply the lessons they are learning.

How to Encourage Participation

Since your Bible study group will consist of Christians at different levels of spiritual maturity, a few may already be familiar with some of the content while for others it will be completely new. Your objective in this Bible study is to help your students win others to the Lord, learn how to build these new Christians in their faith, and train the new believers to introduce others to Christ through small group Bible studies.

Here are some suggestions for encouraging members to participate and for making the discussion time interesting and practical:

- To create a casual, intimate setting, arrange chairs in a circle or sit around a table if you have a small group.
- After reading the Bible passage, invite a member to summarize the passage in his own words before asking any questions about it.
- During the discussion time, avoid embarrassing anyone. When you ask a question of a member, be sure he answers it aptly. If he stumbles, help him along and make him feel that he did answer the question, at least in part. Compliment him on his response.
- When you ask a question, allow time for students to think before continuing. Then listen to their answers rather than mentally planning what you will say next. Remember that you are teaching people, not lessons.
- If you sense confusion about a question you ask, restate it in different words or from another point of view. Define all unusual words.
- Keep the discussion relevant and personal. To redirect the discussion, restate the question or ask for the answers to the next question. If a person asks a question that is off

the topic, tactfully explain that it would be best not to take class time to discuss it. Offer to help answer the question after the study session is over.

- Stimulate conversation by asking questions such as: "What do you think this passage means?" "What can we learn from this passage about God, Christ, ourselves, our responsibilities, our relationships with others?"
- To help students apply the passage personally, ask, "What significance does this have for us today?" "What does this mean to you?" "How does (or will) it affect your life?"
- Often a great deal can be learned by disagreeing over a passage. To keep the discussion from turning into an argument, however, remind everyone that you are studying what the Bible says about a subject. The Bible is your final authority.
- Keep the discussion moving. If you cover the material too quickly, the study will be shallow; if you go too slowly, it will be tedious and boring. The lessons may include more material than you need, so do not spend too much time on any one section, but be sure you cover each major point.
- At the end of the discussion, ask someone to summarize the points that have been made. Be sure to guide the final summary and application.
- Make the group time enjoyable. Allow extra time after each session for social interaction, refreshments, and individual counseling.

Objectives of the Five-Week Study

During this study, your objectives are to help students do the following:

1. **Accept their role in helping to fulfill the Great Commission.** The main purpose of this Bible study is to challenge Christians to reach others for Christ and to understand their part in helping to fulfill the Great Commission.

2. **Learn how to guide new believers to assurance of their salvation.** The five-week Bible study concludes with lessons on how to help your students teach new Christians about their permanent relationship with Jesus Christ and how to walk in the Spirit daily.

3. **Challenge Christians to develop a ministry of spiritual multiplication.** A ministry of discipleship is more than just helping new believers understand the Great Commission. It is also vital to challenge them to win others for Christ and train them to win still others to Christ.

Additional Resources to Help You Lead the Study

To help you lead the study, I recommend using or studying several additional resources. The five lessons in this study use the *Four Spiritual Laws* as a witnessing and follow-up tool. Although you can adapt the lessons to use other evangelistic material, the *Four Spiritual Laws* is a time-tested tool that can help your students become more confident and effective in their witnessing. Order a package of 50 to give to your students and to use in witnessing situations outside the session times.

The lessons also suggest a plan for discipleship called the "Process for Building Multiplying Disciples." (A chart outlining this plan is in Step 2.) This plan gives an excellent outline of how to conduct a discipleship ministry from witnessing through leadership training. This process includes using some or all of the following additional materials in your discipleship ministry:

- *"JESUS"* video (evangelism tool)
- *A Man Without Equal* video and book (evangelism tool)
- *The Joy of Hospitality* book (evangelism and follow-up tool)
- *Jesus and the Intellectual* booklet (evangelism tool)
- *A Great Adventure* booklet (evangelism tool)
- *Reaching Your World Through Witnessing Without Fear* individual video package (evangelism tool)

- *Five Steps of Christian Growth* Bible study curriculum (follow-up tool)
- *Five Steps to Sharing Your Faith* Bible study curriculum (evangelism and follow-up)
- *Five Steps to Making Disciples* Bible study curriculum (follow-up tool)

Other materials may also help you and your students learn how to become effective disciple-makers:

- *Have You Made the Wonderful Discovery of the Spirit-Filled Life?* booklet (follow-up tool)
- *Witnessing Without Fear* book (evangelism study)
- *Leading a Small Group: The Ultimate Road Trip* Bible study curriculum (help for Bible study leaders)
- Transferable Concepts booklets:

  How You Can Introduce Others to Christ (evangelism)
  How You Can Be a Fruitful Witness (evangelism)
  How You Can Help Fulfill the Great Commission (follow-up)
  How You Can Be Sure You Are a Christian (follow-up)
  How You Can Experience God's Love and Forgiveness (follow-up)
  How You Can Be Filled With the Holy Spirit (leadership training)
  How You Can Walk in the Spirit (leadership training)
  How You Can Love By Faith (leadership training)

How to Use the Lesson Plans

To teach this series of lessons effectively, study each part of the lesson before the group meeting. *There is no substitute for preparation.* Studying the lesson thoroughly will enable you to lead the discussion with confidence. If you take shortcuts in your preparation time, your group will not learn the principles effectively.

Prepare for each session by doing the following:

- Pray for the individuals in the group. Keep a list of each person's special needs and refer to it during your personal prayer time.
- Thank God for what He will teach all of you.
- Reread the objectives of the study.
- Review the session outline.
- Study the verses and answers to the questions in each lesson. Since the answers are printed in your Leader's Guide, you may be tempted to skip this step. However, familiarity with the Scripture passages and answers will help you during the group discussion.

Each lesson includes the following main parts:

Focus

This is a summary of the topic covered in the lesson.

Objectives

These are the main goals of the lesson. To help your students meet them and to keep the lesson on track, remember these objectives as you prepare and as you guide the discussion. A helpful technique is to jot the goals in your Leader's Guide where you want to emphasize them.

Session Scriptures

These verses will give you an overview of the material covered in the lesson. You may want to read these verses in your quiet time during the week.

Outline

The outline presents the structure of the Bible study. Use it as a map to help you see where the lesson is heading.

Leader's Preparation

This material is for your enrichment and instruction in presenting the lesson and tells you what to bring to the session. Review this section just before you come to class.

The Bible Study Session

To help you as you guide the lesson, the leader's directions are in bold type, and the answers to questions are in parentheses and italicized.

Sharing

This opening time is designed to help your group share their progress in applying the previous lesson. Relate personal joys and concerns as well as experiences that you or other members of your group have had. Set a friendly, non-threatening tone for the discussion time. Before beginning the lesson, open with prayer, asking the Holy Spirit to guide the study and prepare your hearts for God's Word.

Discussion Starter

Your opening question and the resulting discussion should stimulate thinking, but not necessarily supply answers. Guide the discussion by interjecting further questions. Do not correct wrong answers at this time, but use the discussion to make your students think.

Lesson Development

This section gives directions for leading the Bible study. The ideas will enable you to help group members understand each principle studied. Adapt the teaching suggestions to your group size and personalities and to your leadership style. When reading Scripture passages, use a variety of methods. For example:

- Read the passage aloud while the group follows along.
- Have everyone read it silently.
- Ask a different person to read each verse or passage. (This is preferred.)

- Ask one member to read while the others follow along.

Application

This section will help you challenge your group members to apply what they have learned. Many of the application points should be considered by each member privately. Your role is to guide their thinking and lead them to personal decisions.

Closing and Prayer

This is a good time to ask for any additional comments or questions on the lesson material. Then encourage one of the members to lead the group in prayer. Also use this time to pray for specific needs and concerns expressed by the students.

Follow-Up

This section contains suggestions for helping your group members outside the lesson time and for planning fellowship gatherings. Adapt them for your group's particular situation.

Student Lesson Plan

Located at the end of each lesson, this plan is a duplicate of the Study Guide. Instructions in the Leader's Guide tell when to use the Study Guide material. Encourage members to record their answers in their Study Guides during the group time and refer to them between sessions.

I pray that, during your study, God will open your mind and heart to the truths presented here. As you help others discover the dynamics of spiritual growth, you will see changed lives. While your group may be small, the impact of what you do will multiply in the years ahead as you and your group members follow God's leading into greater ministry and fruitful living.

Answer God's Call to Discipleship

Focus

Each Christian should understand God's call to make disciples, and make a commitment to follow-up new Christians and challenge believers who are more mature in their faith to become disciple-makers.

Objectives

This session will help students to:

- *Study* the example of Jesus in discipleship
- *Understand* the biblical mandate to all Christians to make disciples
- *Accept* their responsibility in following up new Christians
- *Evaluate and deepen* their commitment to the call to make disciples

Session Scriptures

Matthew 28:18–20; Romans 8:9; 1 Corinthians 3:5–9; 9:24–27; 2 Corinthians 2:4; Philippians 1:20,21; 3:8; Colossians 1:24–29; 2 Timothy 4:17,18; Hebrews 13:17

Outline

I. The discipleship ministry of Jesus
II. Example of a disciple-maker
III. Our responsibility
IV. The call to make disciples
V. Answering the call to discipleship

Leader's Preparation

Being a disciple-maker involves a deep commitment to the commands and principles Jesus taught. Therefore, it is essential that you examine or renew your attitudes toward training others to follow Christ.

To help you evaluate your commitment, during your quiet time read the following passages from God's Word that give guidance on how to be an effective disciple-maker. As you meditate on the verses, examine your commitment to building disciples. Ask the Lord to help you pass on to your group members your vision for changing lives. Use the insights you gain in your personal Bible study to help you become a more effective disciple-maker.

- Jesus' examples of servanthood (humbly serve others): John 13:3–15
- The commitment of a disciple (count the cost and follow Jesus): Luke 14:25–33
- Qualities of true discipleship (follow Jesus' commands and love one another as He loves us): John 8:30–32; 13:34,35
- The fruit of a disciple (remain in Christ and He will bear fruit through us): John 15:5–8
- The actions of a disciple (call others to follow Jesus): John 1:35–45
- The faithfulness of a disciple (follow Jesus even if others desert Him): John 6:53–69
- A disciple's reward (experience blessing a hundred times over): Mark 10:28–30

One of the goals of a discipleship ministry is to help others begin to mature in their leadership abilities. This mean getting to know each person in your group so you can train them more effectively. Take time to pray for each person who has agreed to attend your group. Reflect on their spiritual and leadership qualities. What are their strengths? Weaknesses? Which members seem to align most closely with discipleship goals? Create a chart like the one below, filling it out as you progress through the five lessons. Use it to help you direct the lesson material to meet the needs of your group.

Student's Name	Heart for God	Dependence on Holy Spirit	Teachability	Ability to build relationships

During the Bible study, challenge your group members to a deeper commitment to following Christ. Remember that God is the one who helps believers grow in His kingdom, so keep an open mind about how each group member fits into a discipleship ministry. The next session will give you an opportunity to help members find their area of ministry in discipleship.

This Bible study assumes that participants know how to share their faith and use the *Four Spiritual Laws* to help nonbelievers receive Christ through prayer. However, if you or other group members need more training in witnessing, you may want to begin your discipleship Bible study by spending a few sessions working through the *Five Steps to Sharing Your Faith* Bible study as a group. Or, if you have one or two students who need more help in sharing their faith, you could make available the video package *Reaching Your World Through Witnessing Without Fear* for individual study.

Bring 3×5 cards, pencils, and a flip chart to this session.

The Bible Study Session

Sharing (5 minutes)

Greet members warmly as they arrive. Pass out the Study Guides, and ask students to turn to the Contents page. Read through the lesson titles, then say: We are going to begin an adventure that will result in a greater ministry than anything else we could ever do. With a small investment of time and a commitment to following Jesus, we can influence the lives of many people. I am excited about what we will learn and how we can use key information to reach out to others.

Next, distribute the 3×5 cards and pencils. Ask the group members to write their names, addresses, and telephone numbers on one side of the card. Collect the cards, and use them during the five-week study to record prayer requests and needs for each person. If group members do not know each other, have each person briefly introduce himself at this time. To introduce the topic of discipleship, share your commitment to this group.

Discussion Starter (5 minutes)

Read this true story:

Two eighteen-year-olds received Jesus as their personal Savior. One was a professional drummer, the other a football player. Each was deeply entrenched in worldly habits when he came to know Jesus Christ. Neither had a background in God's Word or in Christian behavior.

John, the drummer, was introduced to Christ by a friend who played guitar in his band. Soon afterward, the band was dissolved and John was left on his own. He attended church for a while, but he was a poor reader and found it hard to study the Bible by himself. Within two years, John was heavily involved in drugs and immorality. Today, he continues to wander far from God, though he is still quick to call himself a Christian.

Steve also found his faith exciting at first, but missed his drinking buddies and wanted to go out with them. "Oh, no, you shouldn't," objected the neighbor who had introduced him to Christ. "Let's study the Bible together. You can learn how to introduce your friends to Jesus Christ, too."

The neighbor faithfully shared God's Word with Steve. He encouraged him to pray and introduced him to other Christians. As a result, when Steve graduated from college, he went on to seminary. Today he pastors a thriving church.

Ask:

- What are the differences between the two men's experiences? *(Discipleship; involvement with Christians; a believer who spent time with Steve.)*
- In your opinion, why is discipleship so essential? *(Allow group members to respond freely.)*

Say: To give us an idea of good discipleship skills, we will read a definition of discipleship and then look at how Jesus practiced discipleship. Of course, He is the supreme example of how to conduct a discipleship ministry.

Lesson Development (30–40 minutes)

The Discipleship Ministry of Jesus

Say: A disciple is a follower of Jesus. According to the *Dictionary of Christianity in America*, discipleship "identifies the lifestyle or process whereby individuals or groups live out their understanding of what it mean to be a disciple."[2] Therefore, to clearly understand how to make disciples, we must understand what Jesus taught about discipleship. Jesus considered follow-up so important that He spent His entire ministry working with the people closest to Him. By the time He went back to heaven, He had trained them so well that they began a movement under the power of the Holy Spirit which eventually reached all over the known world.

---

[2] Reid, Daniel, ed., *Dictionary of Christianity in America,* Downers Grove, IL: Intervarsity Press, 1990, p. 357.

Jesus' motive in everything He did was to glorify God. **Read John 17:4.** Jesus was both an example and a teacher. In word and deed, He provided a model for discipleship that His followers are to reproduce in their own ministries. Let's consider principles of Jesus' ministry that will help us effectively disciple others.

On your flip chart, write the three questions in the box. Read the questions and explain that they are to be asked with each of the eight principles given in the Study Guide. (If time does not allow you to ask every question of each passage, select the one or two questions that are most appropriate for each principle.) Then form two to four groups and assign each several principles. After a short time of small-group discussion, reconvene and have each group briefly report what they discussed.

Questions:

1. What other passages in the Gospels (Matthew, Mark, Luke, and John) show how Jesus taught or modeled this characteristic? (Use your Bible's topical index.)
2. What might happen if a disciple-maker taught (only used words) but did not model this principle for new believers? How about if he modeled (only used actions) but did not teach the principle?
3. How can we apply this principle in our own ministries?

Principles Jesus modeled in His discipleship ministry:

1. *Jesus prayed for His disciples* (John 17:9–11). This is our first responsibility to those whom we disciple. Paul also prayed for his disciples (Ephesians 1:15–19). God will use our prayers as well as our model of Christian living in the lives of those we disciple.
2. *Jesus taught them God's Word* (Luke 24:44–48). He quoted Scripture and taught them to understand the Bible.
3. *Jesus depended on God and the power of the Holy Spirit* (John 5:30; Luke 4:1). Even Jesus, the Son of God, submit-

ted Himself to God the Father and walked humbly in the power of the Holy Spirit.

4. *Jesus trained His disciples and sent them out to minister* (Matthew 28:18–20; Mark 3:13,14; Acts 1:8). Jesus began focusing on a few disciples out of the many people who followed Him. Jesus' worldwide mission depended on training and equipping His disciples to reach all people with the gospel, so He modeled a personal ministry to them, then sent them out to apply what they had learned. They in turn could reproduce His ministry and reach the masses after He returned to heaven.

5. *Jesus urged His disciples to take steps of faith* (Matthew 14:22–32). He placed a high value on the faith of His friends. He did not admonish them because of their many ministry mistakes, but He did rebuke them for their lack of faith.

6. *Jesus emphasized an eternal perspective* (Matthew 6:19–21). All that Jesus taught and did pointed to the reality and priority of the unseen, eternal world.

7. *Jesus initiated and modeled evangelism* (Luke 8:1; John 4:27–42). Everywhere Jesus went, He proclaimed the good news of salvation—to large groups or to individuals, to the spiritually receptive and to the hostile.

8. *Jesus was an example of servanthood* (Matthew 20:28; John 13:1–17). Although He was God, Jesus was the servant-leader, putting into action His radical commitment to place the interests and welfare of others before His own, even to the point to death (Philippians 2:8).

Point out the following three questions in the Study Guide. Take a few moments to discuss these questions:

- What is most significant to you about Jesus' discipleship ministry?
- How did Jesus use both words and actions in training others?

- How have you seen this combination work in your ministry?

Then say: Let's look at one good example of a disciple-maker—the apostle Paul.

Example of a Disciple-Maker

Say: Paul is an excellent example of a man living out God's purpose as a disciple-maker. Disciples are followers of Jesus who love and serve Him and, through the power of the Holy Spirit, become increasingly like Him. A disciple calls others to follow Jesus and helps them grow in their faith.

The following passages show characteristics in Paul's life that made him a good disciple-maker. After each reference, write the qualities and how each is displayed in your life. **After reading the passages, give students a few moments to write, then discuss their answers.**

- Romans 8:9; 2 Corinthians 2:4 *(Empowered by the Spirit.)*
- 1 Corinthians 9:24–27 *(Self-disciplined; trained for the job.)*
- Philippians 1:20,21 *(Displayed courage; lived for Christ.)*
- Philippians 3:8 *(Considered everything else worthless compared to knowing Jesus.)*
- Colossians 1:24–29 *(Verse 24: willing to sacrifice for the Church, Christ's body; verse 25: servant spirit in witnessing; verse 28: faithfully proclaimed the gospel to everyone, teaching them about the Lord; verse 28: desired to present believers perfect in the Lord, so he followed up new Christians; verse 29: relied on Christ's power at work within him.)*
- 2 Timothy 4:17,18 *(Dependent on the Lord.)*
- Hebrews 13:17 *(Obedient to authority.)*

Say: Paul displayed many other godly characteristics. I encourage you to study the life of Paul on your own and record all the things he did to further his ministry. **Discuss how Paul's example can be applied today in our ministries.**

Say: God's plan is for His people to use their spiritual knowledge and training to influence others. Let's look at a passage from 1 Corinthians that describes our responsibility in discipling others.

Our Responsibility

Read 1 Corinthians 3:5–9. Discuss the following points regarding our accountability in discipleship and apply them to this passage.

1. *We are God's instruments on earth.* He chooses to work through people to accomplish His purposes. Our obligation is just as great in follow-up as it is in evangelism. Paul recognized that God causes spiritual growth, but he also called himself a co-worker with God. Just as God uses people to bring others to Christ, He uses people to help new believers mature.
2. *We have the privilege and responsibility to nurture new Christians* and create an environment that encourages spiritual growth. Just as the stories of Steve and John show, the loving guidance a new Christian receives from a more mature believer can make a vital difference in his life.

Say: All of us are where we are today in our spiritual growth because of the input of more mature and caring Christians. Perhaps your godly parents, a Sunday school teacher, or a friend helped you grow as a Christian during tough times or challenged you to stretch your faith in some way. **Talk about one or two people who had a positive impact on your Christian growth. Then allow group members to tell about people who influenced their spiritual growth.**

Say: Not everyone we introduce to Christ or challenge to begin a discipleship ministry will follow through with a commitment to making disciples. Remember, ultimately, God is responsible for spiritual growth. We cannot make anyone mature in their faith. Our responsibility is to follow Christ's commands and His example in discipleship and leave the results to God.

The Call to Make Disciples

Say: Jesus calls us to make disciples of others. **Read Matthew 28:18–20 and Colossians 1:28,29.** These two passages are parallel in five main points about the call to make disciples. Let us take a closer look at what it means to "make disciples" of others.

Have the students form pairs. Read the first point, then give pairs 2 or 3 minutes to consider this question: What impact does this point have on my ministry? **Ask students to write their conclusions in their Study Guides, then go on to the next point.**

- *The authority and power are from Jesus*, who has all authority. Everywhere He sends us, He has already established His authority. We minister in Jesus' authority and in His power made available to us by the Holy Spirit. Acts 1:8 tells us that the Holy Spirit will empower us to take the gospel to the ends of the earth. God provides us with all the power we need to do what He calls us to do.
- *The imperative is to disciple others.* We are to accomplish this by going and teaching—but the focus of these passages is on the divine command to "make disciples." God calls us to lead others to Christ and to establish them in their faith as His followers.
- *The scope is the whole world.* The disciples of Jesus are commissioned to win and develop disciples in every part of the human race. We are to teach every person—not just certain people, not just our own "tribe." No place is off limits to making disciples.
- *The task is both evangelism and discipleship.* To make disciples, we must first win them to Christ. We take the initiative to present the gospel to all who will listen. Our goal is to share Christ with as many people as possible, as soon as possible.

  Then, with God's wisdom, we are to teach everyone to obey Christ's commands, including the Great Commission. Evangelism must result in faithful disciples and our faithful disciples must be trained in evangelism. This is a long-term job that can only be done in the power of the Holy Spirit.

- *The expectation is that Jesus will bless us in our work.* As we seek to make disciples, we must anticipate two things: It will require *hard work* in the power of the Holy Spirit. Jesus will *bless us* with His presence. He sends us out to help in a worldwide task, but He will never allow us to minister alone.

For each of the following points, look up the verses and discuss how these characteristics help us in a discipleship ministry. Ask this question after each point: Given this information, what is God asking you to do differently? **Possible discussion material is given for each point.**

- *Love others* (John 13:34,35; Philippians 2:4). Loving one another is the identifying characteristic of disciples of Jesus. We should also consider the needs of others, many times even before our own needs.

- *Obediently apply His Word to our lives* (John 14:23,24; 1 John 5:3). It is not enough to say that you are a Christian or a disciple; you must show it by your attitude and actions in obeying God.

- *Fish for men* (Matthew 4:19). It is impossible to be a disciple of Jesus and not be sharing Him with others (John 15:8).

- *Pray according to God's will* (1 John 5:14,15). Prayer aligns the disciple's heart, mind, and will with the will of our heavenly Father as revealed in His Word.

- *Depend moment by moment on the power of the Holy Spirit* (Acts 1:8; Ephesians 5:18). The Holy Spirit supplies the power that enables a disciple to obey God's commands.

- *Suffer with and for Jesus* (Philippians 1:29,30). Disciples are not above their Master. As the world persecuted and rejected Jesus, it will sometimes persecute and reject His followers. Our willingness to suffer for Him enables us to persevere in serving Him.

Application (10 minutes)

Answering the Call to Discipleship

Say: Now that we have studied the biblical call to make disciples, how committed are you to making disciples? Silently review the questions in the Action Point in your Study Guide as you consider your ministry. Write down ways you will implement changes. **Allow members time to reflect on the Action Point questions.**

1. Am I presently depending on Jesus' power in my life and ministry? How can I deepen this dependence?
2. Do I view making disciples as an imperative in my life and ministry? How can I increase my vision and concern?
3. Does my personal ministry have "reaching the world" as its objective? How can I broaden my ministry?
4. Is my evangelism resulting in faithful disciples and are my faithful disciples being trained in evangelism? In what ways can I allow the Lord to work more fully in me toward these goals?
5. Am I working hard in the power of the Holy Spirit and am I expecting Jesus to bless the work? How can I allow the Holy Spirit to become more effective as He works through me?

When students finish, say: During our next four sessions, we will be learning how all these points fit into a personal ministry. If you are unsure of how to respond to some of these now, jot your questions here, then bring them up at the appropriate time.

Our next lesson introduces us to the most exciting and effective method for reaching our world for Christ—spiritual multiplication. We will also discuss our part in helping to fulfill Jesus' command, the Great Commission.

Closing (5 minutes)

Encourage students to share any commitments they made during the session. Pray for their ability to follow through on their commitments and to build a ministry of discipleship into their lives.

Follow-Up

Follow-up activities for these lessons are very important because they are designed to prepare the student for starting his own discipleship group. To become a multiplying disciple, the first step he must take is to introduce others to Christ. To help your students begin witnessing as a way of life, take them out witnessing with you to learn from your example. You may do this as a part of your church visitation, as you meet with friends who do not know Christ, or as a neighborhood outreach.

During the second session, students will begin learning how to have follow-up appointments with these new believers. By Step 5, the students will be ready to form their own groups.

Student Lesson Plan

The Discipleship Ministry of Jesus

Discuss the principles with your group and write down the most pertinent points.

1. Jesus prayed for His disciples (John 17:9–11).
2. Jesus taught them God's Word (Luke 24:44–48).
3. Jesus depended on God and the power of the Holy Spirit (John 5:30; Luke 4:1).
4. Jesus trained His disciples and sent them out to minister (Matthew 28:18–20; Mark 3:13,14; Acts 1:8).
5. Jesus urged His disciples to take steps of faith (Matthew 14:22–32).
6. Jesus emphasized an eternal perspective (Matthew 6:19–21).
7. Jesus initiated and modeled evangelism (Luke 8:1; John 4:27–42).
8. Jesus was an example of servanthood (Matthew 20:28; John 13:1–17).

Questions for Reflection

- What is most significant to you about Jesus' discipleship ministry?
- How did Jesus use both words and actions in training others?
- How have you seen this combination work in your ministry?

Example of a Disciple-Maker

The following passages show characteristics in Paul's life that made him a good disciple-maker. Write the qualities after each reference. How is each quality displayed in your life?

- Romans 8:9; 2 Corinthians 2:4

- 1 Corinthians 9:24–27
- Philippians 1:20,21
- Philippians 3:8
- Colossians 1:24–29
- 2 Timothy 4:17,18
- Hebrews 13:17

Our Responsibility

How do these points fit in with 1 Corinthians 3:5–9 and our responsibility in disciple-making?

1. We are God's instruments on earth.
2. We have the privilege and responsibility to nurture new Christians and create an environment that encourages spiritual growth.

Not everyone we introduce to Christ or challenge to begin a discipleship ministry will follow through with a commitment to making disciples. Remember, ultimately, God is responsible for spiritual growth. We cannot make anyone mature in their faith. Our responsibility is to follow Christ's commands and His example for discipleship and leave the results to God.

The Call to Make Disciples

Jesus calls us to make disciples of others. Matthew 28:18–20 and Colossians 1:28,29 are parallel in five main points about the call to make disciples. Read each item, then consider this question: What impact does the point have on my ministry? Write your conclusions here:

- The authority and power are from Jesus.
- The imperative is to disciple others.
- The scope is the whole world.
- The task is both evangelism and discipleship.
- The expectation is that Jesus will bless us in our work.

Look up each set of verses and discuss how these characteristics help us in a discipleship ministry. Answer this question for each point: Given this information, what is God asking you to do differently?

- Love others (John 13:34,35; Philippians 2:4).
- Obediently apply His Word to our lives (John 14:23,24; 1 John 5:3).
- Fish for men (Matthew 4:19).
- Pray according to God's will (1 John 5:14,15).
- Depend moment by moment on the power of the Holy Spirit (Acts 1:8; Ephesians 5:18).
- Suffer with and for Jesus (Philippians 1:29,30).

Answering the Call to Discipleship

Action Point: After studying the biblical call to make disciples, how committed are you to making disciples? Silently review these questions as you consider your ministry. Write down ways you will implement changes.

1. Am I presently depending on Jesus' power in my life and ministry? How can I deepen this dependence?
2. Do I view making disciples as an imperative in my life and ministry? How can I increase my vision and concern?
3. Does my personal ministry have "reaching the world" as its objective? How can I broaden my ministry?
4. Is my evangelism resulting in faithful disciples and are my faithful disciples being trained in evangelism?

   In what ways can I allow the Lord to work more fully in me toward these goals?
5. Am I working hard in the power of the Holy Spirit and am I expecting Jesus to bless the work?

   How can I allow the Holy Spirit to become more effective as He works through me?

Begin a Discipleship Ministry

Focus

Understanding spiritual multiplication is essential for helping to fulfill the Great Commission and for beginning a discipleship ministry.

Objectives

This session will help students to:

- *Understand* the concept of spiritual multiplication
- *Express* a desire to maximize his effectiveness through spiritual multiplication
- *Begin* to implement a plan to multiply

Session Scriptures

Matthew 25:14–29; 28:18–20; John 9:4; Acts 1:8; Romans 3:10–18; Ephesians 5:15–17; Philippians 2:13; 2 Timothy 2:1–10

Outline

I. The meaning of spiritual multiplication
II. The elements of spiritual multiplication
III. The motivation for spiritual multiplication
IV. Our potential impact
V. Beginning a discipleship ministry

Leader's Preparation

Christianity is alive after two thousand years because Christians have multiplied themselves spiritually. Note the context of Paul's statement in 2 Timothy 2:2. This is not just a casual statement regarding the passing on of a heritage. Paul exhorts Timothy to multiply his faith because persecution is threatening Christianity's survival. In other words, Paul is saying, "Timothy, I'm in jail. I don't know how long I will be on this earth because our enemies will be happy only when the gospel is silenced forever. So the things I have given to you, entrust to faithful men who will teach others. In this way, Christ's message will never die."

The influence of one person who follows the Lord is immeasurable. One believer could set off a chain reaction that eventually affects every corner of a campus or community. One student! One businessman! One employee! One parent! The spiritual concept that enables us through the power of the Holy Spirit to have such an impact is what I call spiritual multiplication. (This concept, which is the focus of this lesson, is explained in "The Principle of Spiritual Multiplication" on page 7.)

Take time to consider what your community would look like if this chain reaction occurred. During the Closing of this session, give your students a picture of what could happen if spiritual multiplication spread throughout your area.

This lesson presents a strategy for spiritual multiplication called "Win, Build, Train, Send," which uses other materials in the *Five Steps* series. Although I encourage you to use the other materials in your discipleship ministry, you may either use this strategy as it is presented in the lesson or modify it for your particular situation.

Bring a flip chart and a world map to this session.

The Bible Study Session

Sharing (5 minutes)

Ask each person to describe his commitment to making disciples. Then talk about the kind of influence your group might have in the lives of others around you. Explain that this lesson will give an even greater perspective on the influence one Christian can have for Christ.

Discussion Starter (5 minutes)

Say: When using mathematical functions, a number grows much faster through multiplication than through addition. Let's try a demonstration that dramatically proves this principle. **Ask members to first *add* the number 4 ten times (4+4+4+4+4+4+4+4+4+4=40). Then ask students to *multiply* the number 4 ten times (4×4×4×4×4×4×4×4×4×4=1,048,576). Discuss the difference in results between addition and multiplication.**

Say: The same principle applies to spiritual addition and spiritual multiplication. This relates directly to our goal to make disciples. Let's find out what spiritual multiplication means.

Lesson Development (20–30 minutes)

The Meaning of Spiritual Multiplication

Explain: In the last session, we learned that Jesus calls us to be His disciples and to make disciples of others. Included in this call is the command to take the gospel to the whole world. **Read Acts 1:8.** But how do we reach the world? It seems like an impossible task.

Say: To reach the maximum number of people for Jesus Christ, we must use spiritual multiplication instead of spiritual addition. In spiritual *addition*, one person leads someone to the Lord, then leads someone else to Him, adding believers to the kingdom of God one by one. In spiritual *multiplication*, a person introduces a nonbeliever to Jesus, then trains the new Christian to share his faith. Then the more mature Christian and the new believer each introduce someone to Christ. As the process continues and expands, the result is spiritual multiplication.

Say: Many tremendous things are happening in God's work all over the world. Let me read a couple of stories that show how a group such as ours can have a spiritual impact through discipleship.

Read:

From the United States

A Christian woman challenged two young college women she was discipling to begin a Bible study of their own. The women she was training accepted the challenge.

One of the young women invited six people to the first session. Four of the group members were already at her home when the doorbell rang again. The group leader answered the door and was greeted by a magazine saleswoman.

Since the group members were waiting for other members to arrive, the group leader invited the saleswoman to come in. After listening to her presentation and purchasing a magazine, the group leader asked, "Since we've listened to you, will you let me share something with you?"

When the saleswoman nodded, the group leader began sharing the *Four Spiritual Laws*. Soon, the other two members arrived, and everyone had an opportunity to be part of sharing their faith with the saleswoman. To their joy, she received Jesus as her Savior.

Then the doorbell rang again. Another saleswoman stood at the door ready to sell them the same products. She noticed her friend inside the room. "Bonnie!" she exclaimed. "Why are you here? You're supposed to be in another area!"

The group members were excited to see how God's timing had led Bonnie to them through a mistake in defining sales areas.

From Cambodia

In Siem Riep, Cambodia, *"JESUS"* film teams showed the *"JESUS"* video to the neighbors and friends of a group of Cambodian believers. (*"JESUS"* is a re-creation of the ministry, death, and resurrection of Jesus taken from the Gospel of Luke.) The Cambodian Christians trained these new believers to also show the video. Early in the year, one church had 100 members. Within eight months, as trained church members witnessed and showed the video, the church grew to 500 members meeting in ten locations!

The Elements of Spiritual Multiplication

Say: God has given us specific instructions on how to have a ministry of spiritual multiplication. **Read 2 Timothy 2:1–10.** Let's discuss two elements of spiritual multiplication found in verses 1 and 2. **Encourage members to take notes in their Study Guides.**

1. *The power for spiritual multiplication* (verse 1). God never calls us to a task without first giving us the power to accomplish it. His work, done in His power by His means, will always bear fruit that remains.

   Be strong—Paul urged Timothy to be strengthened by Jesus as he built a ministry of spiritual multiplication. Paul is saying, "Timothy, you will need to rely on Christ's strength if you are to succeed in this type of ministry." We, too, will need Christ's strength to keep going, especially when we do not feel like continuing on.

   In the grace that is in Christ Jesus—Paul encouraged Timothy to remember the grace of Jesus as his source of power for ministry. Timothy would find this strength in the fact that Jesus extended unmerited favor to him even though as a sinner he did not deserve it. We, too, should remember that only through grace can we accomplish our work.

2. *The pattern for spiritual multiplication* (verse 2). The pattern of multiplication given in this verse includes four generations: Paul; Timothy; his disciples, the reliable men; and others. **Refer to the diagram in the Study Guide as you discuss this point.**

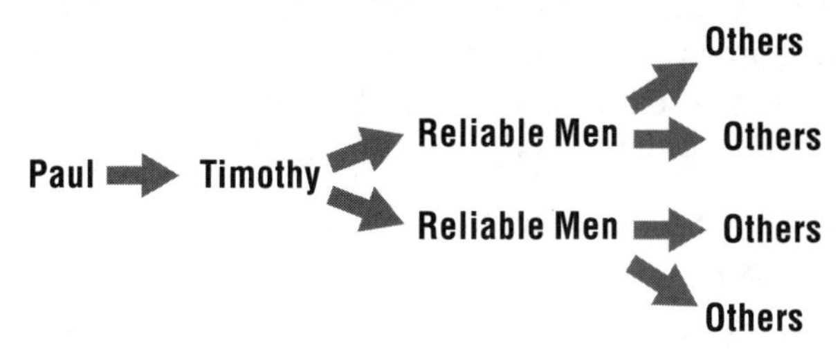

Be taught—The first link in a spiritual multiplication chain is our willingness to be taught. The question "Am I teachable?" is the most important one we can ask. If we continue to be teachable, God can use us in the lives of others.

Entrust to reliable men—We do not entrust worthless items to someone's care, so "the things you have heard me say" are of great value. They are God's life-changing truths, meant to be shared with as many people as possible, who will then share them with others.

Teach others—Find reliable disciples who are qualified to teach others. Multiplying disciples actively seek out others who will continue to pass on this valuable information.

Discuss the following questions in the Study Guide:

- What promises does Jesus give in Matthew 28:18–20? *(He has the authority to send us; He will be with us always.)*
- Why are the promises so significant? *(He provides His power for us; we do not go alone.)* **Say:** Not only does God promise to be with us, but the Father, Son, and Holy Spirit are all directly involved in making disciples.
- Since it is God's will for you to make disciples, how does the promise in Philippians 2:13 relate to this command? *(God works in us to make disciples; we do not do it in our own strength or wisdom.)*

The Motivation for Spiritual Multiplication

Say: In the 2 Timothy passage, Paul uses three professions—soldier, athlete, and farmer—to illustrate the perspective of a spiritual multiplier. Each occupation has something to teach us about the kind of character and commitment it takes to meet the challenges found in a multiplication ministry. **Ask:**

- How is a spiritual multiplier similar to a soldier? *(Allow for responses.)*

Explain: The mindset of a soldier typifies at least two essential characteristics of a successful spiritual multiplier: being single-minded and being willing to suffer hardship. The good soldier knows not to involve himself in civilian affairs so he can focus on pleasing his commanding officer. He also knows how to endure on the front lines to help win the battle.

In a similar way, spiritual multipliers keep their focus not on the things of the world, but on making disciples in spite of personal cost. Their motivation is to please the Lord. They realize that they are in a battle for men's souls and keep working despite weariness. **Ask:**

- How does a spiritual multiplier resemble an athlete? *(Allow for responses.)*

Explain: An athlete models at least two essential characteristics of a spiritual multiplier: he is trained to compete and he follows the rules.

The victorious athlete disciplines himself to compete at the highest level. He knows that behind every victory lies hours of rigorous training. He also knows the rules of the game and plays accordingly.

Spiritual multipliers discipline themselves to achieve victory over sin and apply themselves to making disciples. They also learn God's rules and follow them. **Ask:**

- How is a spiritual multiplier illustrated by a farmer? *(Allow for responses.)*

Explain: There are two essential characteristics of a spiritual multiplier that a farmer exemplifies: he works hard and enjoys a fruitful harvest.

The successful farmer is not afraid of manual labor that results in a fruitful harvest. His patience and hard work through rain and hot sun are rewarded when he brings in the crop.

In a similar way, a spiritual multiplier spends long hours sowing and cultivating the Word of God, which is sometimes physically exhausting. But he sees a harvest of people who are won to Christ and discipled.

Give the following three motivational factors as you write them on your flip chart. Invite students to take notes in their Study Guides under the heading "The Motivation for Spiritual Multiplication." Say: In 2 Timothy 2:8–10, Paul points out three motivational factors for the spiritual multiplier: 1) the example of our Lord Jesus Christ; 2) the Word of God; and 3) a burden for the lost. **Ask:**

- What might happen to your ministry if any of these are missing? *(Allow for responses.)*

Say: Our greatest motivation is to respond to God's love for us. Because He loved us enough to make us part of His kingdom, we want to help as many others as possible find His love and forgiveness, too. We want them to experience the peace and joy that we have found.

Although not all Christians will be faithful to the task, God calls all of us to be His disciples and to make disciples of others. There are three reasons it is so essential to participate in the urgent, worldwide mission of building spiritual multipliers: **Write these points on your flip chart as you give them. Encourage students to record the points in their Study Guides.**

1. *The spiritual needs of the world* (Romans 3:10–18). The Bible tells us that all men have sinned and no one is righteous. These verses give us a picture of how desperate the world's condition is and how much it needs Christ. **Ask:**
   - What world events illustrate how desperately wicked and far from God our world is? *(Allow for responses.)*
2. *The urgency of the hour* (John 9:4). In the amount of time this session takes, many people will enter eternity without Christ. Thousands of people will be born but only a few will become Christians. **Ask:**
   - If someone asked you, how would you explain to them why spiritual multiplication is so strategic? *(We don't know how long the door of opportunity will remain open in each area; eternal destinies are at stake; God tells us to*

do it right now; it is the most effective method for reaching the world.)

3. *The scope of the task* (Matthew 28:19; Acts 1:8). **Hold up the world map to emphasize the scope of our task in light of the urgency of the hour. Then ask:**

   - How would you describe the scope of the task? *(The entire world needs a Savior; we have more than 5 billion people to reach.)*

If you know of missionaries involved in a discipleship ministry, point out the areas in which they serve and describe their impact. Emphasize that our ministry goes further than just our local area as we financially support and pray for these Christians.

Our Potential Impact

Say: Spiritual multiplication has a strategic, long-term impact built into it. It is more than having an influence, but having a *maximum* impact. To give you an idea of what one person can do, let me show you a diagram. **Review the principle of mathematical progression and refer to the Spiritual Multiplication diagram below. For added effect, draw a circle on your flip chart and write "YOU" in the center. Then expand the diagram by adding multiplied circles as you give the following illustration:**

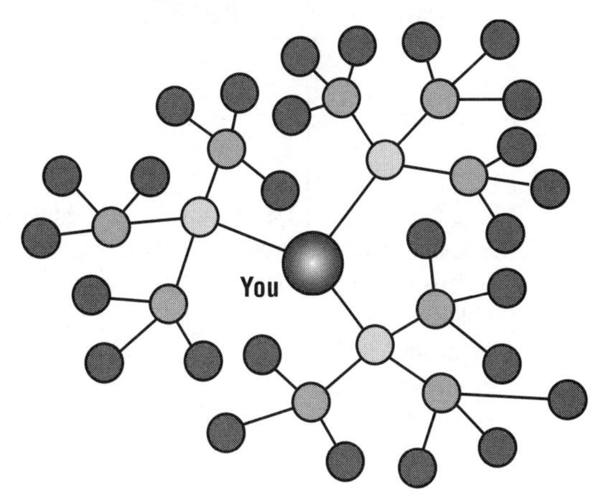

Let me show you how rapidly our diagram would expand if we practiced spiritual multiplication. If you consistently train three disciples each year and each of your disciples consistently train their own three disciples each year, you would begin a multiplication chain. After only twenty years, your multiplication chain would have more than 3.5 billion people in small groups (spiritual multiplication). On the other hand, it would take 250,000 *years* to talk to 3.5 billion people if you personally witnessed to 14,000 people a day (spiritual addition). As you can easily see, it is impossible to talk to 14,000 people a day, but we *can* disciple three people a year who would go on to disciple three more people each year.

The point of this illustration is not the specific numbers. None of us will ever have a multiplication chain of 3.5 billion people. But, given the potential of spiritual multiplication, we would be foolish to ignore it or fail to place emphasis on it as we help fulfill the Great Commission.

Having a game plan for implementing spiritual multiplication is essential. The following strategy is built around the *Five Steps* series that we are using. This strategy is called "Win, Build, Train, Send." **Go over the following chart, which is also in the Study Guide.**

Process for Building Multiplying Disciples				
	Part 1	**Part 2**	**Part 3**	**Part 4**
PRINCIPLE	Win	Build	Train	Send
METHOD	Present the gospel, evangelism	Follow-up appointments and Christian growth Bible study: new Christians learn assurance of salvation and walking in power of Holy Spirit	Discipleship groups: members learn to witness	Multiplication groups: members start their own groups

Process for Building Multiplying Disciples *(continued)*				
	Part 1	**Part 2**	**Part 3**	**Part 4**
MATERIALS	*Four Spiritual Laws*, "*JESUS*" video, *A Man Without Equal* video and book, *Jesus and the Intellectual* or *A Great Adventure* booklets	*Five Steps of Christian Growth* Bible study	*Five Steps to Sharing Your Faith* Bible study or *Reaching Your World* video series	*Five Steps to Making Disciples* Bible study
TRAINING LEVEL	Basic training	Intermediate training	Advanced training	Leadership training

Say: Very few people have had the privilege of receiving the training we are receiving right now; therefore, God expects us to use this training for His glory. Our call is clearly to a ministry of spiritual multiplication. **Ask:**

- Although many discipleship methods are effective, why is spiritual multiplication so strategic? *(Every ministry to which God calls us is significant; every part of the body of Christ plays a crucial role in God's work, but not every ministry is equally focused on world evangelization; not all ministries are equal in their long-term impact, but spiritual multiplication will have an effect for generations.)*

Say: As God calls us to reach others and train them, He also calls us to be wise stewards of our resources, ministry opportunities, and time. **Read Matthew 25:14–29. Ask:**

- Why does God consider our stewardship so necessary? *(He owns all that we possess; He gives us everything we have to manage for His purposes.)*

- How does the "Win, Build, Train, Send" process of training fit into stewardship? *(It is part of the abilities and training that God has given us to manage; God expects us to use our training wisely.)*

Read Ephesians 5:15–17. Ask:

- How does God regard the use of our time? *(We should use it wisely; we should make the most of our opportunities.)*

Say: God calls us to make our years here on earth productive for His kingdom. Wherever God calls you will be the most strategic place for you. But God's call on our lives involves being wise stewards of our time, energy, and talents, which enables us to make the most of every opportunity. Spiritual multiplication is a biblical and wise application of our call to make a strategic contribution to our urgent, worldwide mission.

Give this challenge: We have seen the importance God places on discipleship and on the wise use of our resources. A ministry of multiplication is not the only method of helping to fulfill the Great Commission, but it is one that deserves our serious consideration. Making and training disciples through small group Bible studies is an excellent way to maximize the training you are receiving. I urge you to make spiritual multiplication a priority in your life.

Application (10 minutes)

Beginning a Discipleship Ministry

Ask the group to identify ways they can become involved in spiritual multiplication. If they have trouble thinking of any, suggest: praying for Christians to disciple; witnessing; learning how to follow-up a new believer; starting a small group Bible study.

Say: During the next three lessons, we will be learning how to follow-up new believers. To get the most out of the study, I encourage you to begin planning your discipleship ministry now. The first step is to be actively sharing your faith with unbelievers. Some of those you introduce to Christ will become part of your spiritual multiplication chain as you train them to share their faith. Evangelism is the Win part of the strategy. Also, Christians who are not discipling others can also be part of your chain as you challenge them to participate in this thrilling strategy. In our next lessons, we'll be implementing the Build, Train, and Send parts of the strategy.

If any of your group members feel hesitant about sharing their faith, you may want to suggest evangelism training. Either encourage individual students to go through the *Reaching Your World Through Witnessing Without Fear* video or you may want to suspend this study for a few weeks while your group goes through the *Five Steps to Sharing Your Faith* Bible study. If your students feel confident about sharing their faith using the *Four Spiritual Laws* or are already actively witnessing, go on to the Action Point.

Discuss the questions under the Action Point in the Study Guide, and challenge each person to use the *Four Spiritual Laws* to share the gospel with an unbelieving friend this week. Offer to go along with them.

Closing and Prayer (2–3 minutes)

Share your vision of how your group could influence your community for Christ and mention the opportunities available for your students. Then pray for the group's effectiveness in multiplying themselves spiritually.

Follow-Up

As you accompany your group members on their witnessing appointments, use the time to discuss ideas on being involved in spiritual multiplication, and share what is happening in your area and how the student might fit in. Meeting individually with each student will give you insight as to which ones are ready to move into Steps 3 through 5.

Student Lesson Plan

The Elements of Spiritual Multiplication

Read 2 Timothy 2:1–10. Note the elements of spiritual multiplication found in verses 1 and 2.

1. The power for spiritual multiplication (verse 1)
2. The pattern for spiritual multiplication (verse 2)

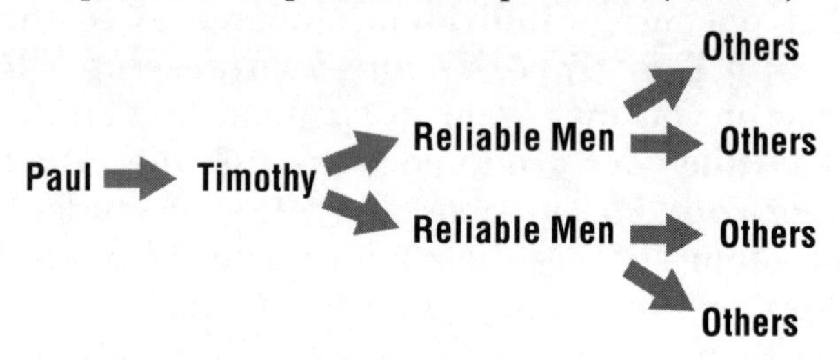

- What promises does Jesus give in Matthew 28:18–20?
- Why are the promises so significant?
- Since it is God's will for you to make disciples, how does the promise in Philippians 2:13 relate to this command?

The Motivation for Spiritual Multiplication

1.
2.
3.

Our motivation to disciple:

Why do we serve as disciplers? Fill in the following points:

1. Romans 3:10–18
2. John 9:4
3. Matthew 28:19; Acts 1:8

Our Potential Impact

This diagram gives you an idea of what one person can do.

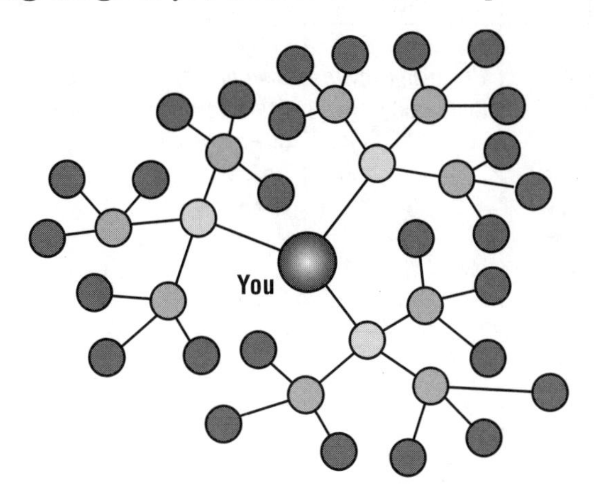

The following chart gives an effective method for multiplying spiritually.

Process for Building Multiplying Disciples				
	Part 1	**Part 2**	**Part 3**	**Part 4**
PRINCIPLE	Win	Build	Train	Send
METHOD	Present the gospel, evangelism	Follow-up appointments and Christian growth Bible study: new Christians learn assurance of salvation and walking in power of Holy Spirit	Discipleship groups: members learn to witness	Multiplication groups: members start their own groups

Process for Building Multiplying Disciples *(continued)*				
	Part 1	**Part 2**	**Part 3**	**Part 4**
MATERIALS	*Four Spiritual Laws*, *"JESUS"* video, *A Man Without Equal* video and book, *Jesus and the Intellectual* or *A Great Adventure* booklets	*Five Steps of Christian Growth* Bible study	*Five Steps to Sharing Your Faith* Bible study or *Reaching Your World* video series	*Five Steps to Making Disciples* Bible study
TRAINING LEVEL	Basic training	Intermediate training	Advanced training	Leadership training

Action Point: The areas in my community that the Lord is laying on my heart to influence for Christ are:

As a result of studying spiritual multiplication in God's Word, I want to take the following steps:

1. *Witness:* As an act of faith, I will commit this week to share my faith in Christ with an unbelieving friend.

   Name: ______________________________

2. *Discipleship group:* To begin my ministry of discipleship, I will begin asking God to bring people whom I can disciple into a discipleship group. I will begin praying for the people I list here:

   ____

   ____

   ____

   ____

Establish Personal Relationships

Focus

We need to discover the importance of follow-up, and learn how to make a follow-up appointment, build personal relationships, and motivate new believers to become involved in the discipleship process.

Objectives

This session will help students to:

- *Understand* the need for basic follow-up
- *Identify* the principles of follow-up
- *Learn* how to make a follow-up appointment

Session Scriptures

Mark 4:3–8,14–20; Acts 1:8; 2:41,42,46; 11:25,26; 20:17–38; 1 Corinthians 3:6,7; Ephesians 5:18; Philippians 1:6; 2:13; Colossians 4:12; 2 Timothy 2:2; Hebrews 10:24,25; 2 Peter 3:18

Outline

I. Basics of follow-up
II. The response to follow-up
III. Paul's example of follow-up
IV. Making a follow-up appointment

Leader's Preparation

Several of the passages listed in the Session Scriptures are biblical examples of follow-up. They reveal some of the early disciples' experiences in motivating new believers to grow in their relationship with the Lord and in teaching them to depend on God and to carry Christ's message to the world. Use the following passages as a study before the next session. Write down any points that are significant to you or your group.

- Acts 2:41,42: Peter's influence in Jerusalem
- Acts 17:10–17: Paul's persistence in evangelism and discipleship
- Acts 18:7–11: Paul's efforts in Derbe
- Acts 19:1–10,21,22: Paul's work in Asia
- Ephesians 1:15–23: Paul's intense desire for believers to experience spiritual growth
- Ephesians 3:16–19: Paul's prayer for believers to know Christ's love
- 1 Thessalonians 1:2–10: Paul, Silas, and Timothy's prayer of thanks for their disciples' faithfulness
- 1 Thessalonians 2:7–12: Paul's conduct among the newly established believers

Paul modeled his walk with God before his disciples. He was gentle and caring (1 Thessalonians 2:7), and he loved them (verse 8). His first concern was for the new Christian's welfare, even if that meant sacrifice and hard work for himself (verse 2). This is love in action.

First Thessalonians 2:8 tells us that Paul shared not only the gospel with them, but also his life. He lived a holy, righteous, and blameless life (verse 10). He encouraged, comforted, and exhorted his disciples (verse 12). He prayed for them (Ephesians 1 and 3). These are the qualities a discipler desires to produce in his own life through the power of the Holy Spirit. This lesson will help prepare you and your students to begin a godly discipleship process.

Before leading this session, read "Making a Follow-Up Appointment," which is included in this lesson. The purpose of this appointment is to follow-up new believers after a witnessing situation. Using the Dialog Example at the end of this lesson, practice demonstrating the method with a partner until you can present it with confidence before your Bible study group. You may ask a group member to be your demonstration partner or ask a Christian friend who will agree to attend this session.

This session refers to using the *Four Spiritual Laws* in witnessing situations. Bring enough copies for each student. You may also want to have some available for your students to use outside class time. Bring your flip chart to this session.

The Bible Study Session

Sharing (5 minutes)

Invite your students to express their questions and misgivings about the discipleship process. Help them encourage each other to let God work in their lives right where they are.

Begin by saying: Even the most committed Christians sometimes feel inadequate for the task of discipleship. They may be thinking, *I'm not strong enough in my faith to help others grow in theirs. I have so many faults and weaknesses, how can I be a leader? My skills in dealing with people aren't that great, so how can I build close relationships? I don't know many nonbelievers or new Christians. How can I start a discipleship group?* Have you ever felt this way? What can we do about these doubts?

Discuss how the following points fit into the discipleship process and how they affect the way your students think about discipleship:

- God is not looking for perfect people. He uses those who are available and willing to do His will. God wants our availability, not our ability.
- God uses our weaknesses to display His glory and strength. He doesn't call the qualified, He qualifies the called so that others can see Him at work in us.

- Disciples want to see a Christian leader who is growing in his faith and gaining victory our his sin, not just a person who seems to have it all together.
- Encountering hard times, working through problems, and admitting faults help bring people together. A "perfect environment" does not challenge people to become stronger in God's power.

Discussion Starter (5–8 minutes)

Tell this story:

> Terry sat next to Jack at lunch and read through the *Four Spiritual Laws* booklet with him. Jack received Christ as they prayed together. Terry had to leave immediately after the lunch hour was over. Jack was excited about his decision to follow Christ, but later when he went home, questions began to come to his mind. *What happens now? How can I get to know God better? What if I sin? Will I have to ask Christ to forgive me and invite Him into my life again? What should I do now?*

Discuss with your group: Jack realized that he needed help in finding answers. If you had been Terry, what would you have told Jack? What would you have done differently? *(To answer Jack's questions, Terry could have: set up an appointment to meet later; emphasized that salvation is by faith, not works; reassured him that all of his sins are forgiven; related a few principles of growth such as reading the Bible, praying, having fellowship with other believers, and witnessing; showed him Hebrews 13:5 and assured him that Christ will never leave him.)*

Discuss: Following up new believers is vital to their growth in Christ. Follow-up allows us to build relationships with new Christians that will help them begin their walk with the Lord and catch the vision for becoming multiplying disciples. **Ask:**

- What is one way that a spiritual relationship with another Christian has changed your life?
- What difference does having a spiritual relationship with a more mature Christian make to a new believer?

Lesson Development (30–40 minutes)

Basics of Follow-Up

Read the following definition of follow-up, which is also in the Study Guide:

> Follow-up is the process by which new believers are established in the faith and equipped with the basics of Christianity so they can grow toward spiritual maturity and become multiplying disciples.

Explain: Follow-up lays the foundation upon which new believers grow. These are the basic steps in follow-up:

As you give the following points, read the passages and discuss the part each plays in effective follow-up. Encourage students to take notes in their Study Guides.

1. *Remember that God causes the spiritual growth* (1 Corinthians 3:6,7; Philippians 1:6; 2:13). God is responsible for spiritual growth. We have the privilege of making ourselves available to Him as He works through us. **Describe how putting the responsibility for someone else's growth on God's shoulders has helped you as a leader.**

2. *Build relationships with new believers* (Acts 2:41,42,46). Create an environment of love, encouragement, and friendship. Show new believers that you care about them personally by listening to what they have to say. Spend time with them; do fun things together; find out about their lives; share your life with them. **Give an example of how you have built a friendship with a new Christian.**

3. *Motivate new believers to grow spiritually* (2 Peter 3:18). Encourage them to establish confidence in God's holy Word as the basis for their faith. Then help them continue to grow in their relationship to God by showing how Christ can help them with their needs. This is why listening is so essential. As you listen, you become aware of problems or needs in their lives. Help new believers find answers in the Bible or explain to them how Christ met a

similar need in your life. **Share a personal example of how Christ met a need in your life.**

4. *Introduce new believers to God's desire for all Christians to witness* (Acts 1:8). Then help them understand their responsibility to help others they introduce to Christ grow as disciples who in turn witness and disciple others.

5. *Encourage new Christians to become involved with other believers* (Hebrews 10:24,25). Having a network of Christian friends who are growing in their faith will encourage and strengthen new believers. Introduce them to other Christians as soon as possible. Offer to take them to church and other activities. **Ask volunteers to share how having Christian friends has helped them grow spiritually.**

6. *Pray regularly for those you follow-up* (Colossians 4:12). Prayer is a crucial part of spiritual growth. Not only will the new believer grow as you pray for him, but you will find your prayer life expanding as well. **Discuss how prayer unites those who pray for each other.**

7. *Meet regularly with new believers and teach them how to live Spirit-filled lives* (Acts 11:25,26; Ephesians 5:18). Barnabas and Saul (later called Paul) met with the church in Antioch for a whole year. Among these people were many new Christians. Paul also gives God's command to us to be filled with the Spirit.

8. *Challenge new believers and more mature Christians to become multiplying disciples* (2 Timothy 2:2). The last step in the discipleship process is to help others catch a vision for multiplying themselves spiritually and helping to fulfill the Great Commission.

Say: These steps of follow-up are part of the discipleship process. We have already discussed the first one, God's responsibility in the growth process. In this lesson and the next two lessons, we will apply each of the remaining steps.

Ask students to turn to the Win, Build, Train, Send chart in the previous lesson. Then explain: Just as evangelism (introducing people to Jesus Christ) is the Win part of the discipleship process, follow-up includes the Build, Train, and Send parts of the process. Each step is vital in making disciples who reproduce spiritually. Before we talk about how to begin a relationship with a new believer, let's turn back to Step 3 and read the purpose statement for follow-up.

Ask a volunteer to read the purpose statement for follow-up:

> Christ sends us out to introduce others to Him, to help them become His disciples, and to teach them how to reach out to others (Matthew 28:18–20).

Say: In our last session, we began the Win, or evangelism, step of the discipleship process when we made plans to witness. **Ask volunteers to share about their witnessing experiences.** At times, all of us have had disappointing results when witnessing. **If a member just shared about a situation that did not turn out as expected, mention that here or give one from your own experiences.** Encountering difficult witnessing situations is not unexpected. However, successful witnessing is sharing the gospel in the power of the Holy Spirit and leaving the results to God. In every part of the discipleship process—including evangelism—God is sovereign in the work of making disciples.

Read Philippians 1:6; 2:13. God began the work in the Philippian Christians, and He ensured their growth and fruitfulness through various means. God gives us the desire and the ability to please Him. No amount of time or effort or anything we can do will ensure that those we witness to will receive Christ and go on to maturity. But you can be confident that in His way and in His time, God will accomplish what He has begun in your life and in the lives of others as you are faithful to do what He has called us to do. What we consider failure is part of that process. We must put the results in His hands and just follow His guidance in our discipleship ministry.

You will find that God uses various means to bring about spiritual maturity in your life, including people, events, His Word, and circumstances. He deals with each of us in a unique way. Sometimes the greatest lessons we learn will come from the most trying circumstances. **Ask:**

- What examples can you give from your life illustrating that God produces spiritual growth in unexpected ways?
- How has God dealt with you in a unique way to further your ministry?

Say: Part of our spiritual growth is to learn to handle many different types of ministry situations with a godly spirit. To help us have a clear perspective, God's Word tells us what to expect as we share the Good News with others. Let's look at what the Bible says about the response of unbelievers.

The Response to Follow-Up

Say: Because God gave man a free will to choose to follow or reject Him, He allows people to respond differently to His Word. As we read this passage, remember that the seed is the Word of God. **Read Mark 4:3–8,14–20. Ask:** What were the different responses to God's Word?

During your discussion of the different responses, bring out these points and write them on your flip chart:

1. *(Verse 15: Some people do not accept the Word at all.)*
2. *(Verses 16,17: Some receive the Word superficially, then when problems come they fall away and lose interest.)*
3. *(Verses 18,19: Some hear and respond to the message, but allow it to be crowded out by things of the world.)*
4. *(Verse 20: Some hear, accept God's Word, and bear fruit.)*

Say: Note that the seed, God's Word, was the same in each case. In follow-up, as in witnessing, we are not responsible for the way people react, just how we present the message and love the people we contact. **In each of the following questions, give an example from your own ministry if possible, but keep your comments general. Do not mention names or describe situations so completely that your students can identify the person. Ask:**

- What situations in follow-up may resemble the seed in #2? *(Some people who begin the discipleship process may quit when they encounter difficult circumstances or when the training becomes more rigorous.)*
- What situations in follow-up may resemble the seed in #3? *(Some people who begin the discipleship process may allow other activities to crowd out their desire to grow spiritually and make disciples.)*

Say: We must not be discouraged if some people do not respond as we would like. As in the seed in #4, God will bring into our lives people who will go on to bear much fruit. They will be a joy to us and an encouragement to our ministry. **Give an example from your experience if appropriate.**

The apostle Paul was a great example in follow-up, yet not all those he introduced to Christ became disciple-makers. In fact, Paul was beaten and stoned for sharing his faith and often he had to correct Christians who had become distracted from following Christ. But Paul was very effective in his ministry. The new churches he founded spread the gospel all over the then-known world. Let us look at how he followed up new believers.

Paul's Example of Follow-Up

Say: The apostle Paul was committed to follow-up because the love of Christ compelled him (2 Corinthians 5:14). He spent many hours teaching new believers and encouraging people he had introduced to the Lord. Later in the Book of Acts, he visited the Ephesian Christians. He knew this would be the last time he would see them in this lifetime. His parting words were a review of his ministry philosophy. **Read Acts 20:17–38 verse by verse. After each verse, discuss what Paul said or did that is important to us in following up new believers. Also discuss how we can follow his example. Here are some suggested answers:**

v.17: *(Paul gathered the elders of the church to give them final instructions. To the end of his life, he was concerned about his disciples. We need to have the same concern for our disciples.)*

v.18: *(Paul reminded the Ephesians of his past work. Our lives need to be an open book to others for encouragement and instruction.)*

v.19: *(Paul had a great passion for serving the Lord, despite the hardships he endured. We can commit ourselves to that same passion, which will help us through setbacks and discouragements in ministry.)*

v.20: *(Paul shared the Word of God openly and often. We should share our faith as a way of life, too.)*

v.21: *(Paul shared his faith with all kinds of people. Since Jesus died for all of us, we should have a burden for all people.)*

v.22: *(Paul was led by the Spirit and trusted God to direct his life. We are commanded to be filled with the Spirit and abide in Christ.)*

v.23: *(Paul expected opposition to his ministry, and he sacrificed for his faith. We can prepare ourselves to encounter obstacles to our ministry.)*

v.24: *(Sharing the gospel was more important to Paul than his own life. Like Paul, we can make it our greatest desire to testify of God's grace.)*

v.25: *(Paul was able to put their spiritual welfare in God's hands when he had to leave. We can be confident that God will keep on working in our friends' lives when we are no longer available to do follow-up with them.)*

v.26: *(Paul was saying that by warning unbelievers about God's judgment and telling them of God's love, he had fulfilled what God called him to do.)*

v.27: *(Paul preached all of God's Word, not just the parts people wanted to hear. We can be faithful to teach all of God's Word, too.)*

v.28: *(Paul encouraged his friends to watch over new believers. We can also train others to do follow-up.)*

v.29: *(Paul was aware that his disciples faced opposition from deceivers. We can pray for those we follow-up and help prepare them to handle these kinds of situations in Christ's power.)*

v.30: *(Paul warns them that some of their own number will be deceivers. We can expect this and not be discouraged when people we thought were dedicated to Christ turn away.)*

v.31: *(Paul's burden for them continued for years. Paul was consistent and faithful to his disciples. We can have the same burden for those we disciple.)*

v.32: *(Paul prayed for his disciples. He was confident that God would work in their lives and that His Word would help them grow spiritually. We can have the same confidence when we pray for those we are following up.)*

v.33: *(Paul kept his focus on his ministry goal, not on any personal benefit he might have received. We can constantly guard against focusing on earthly rewards for our ministry.)*

v.34: *(Paul was upright in his financial affairs. We can be good stewards of what God has given us.)*

v.35: *(Paul was an example in giving. We can make giving of our time, talents, and treasure a priority in our lives and teach new believers to do the same.)*

v.36: *(Paul prayed with his friends. We can make prayer an important part of working with the people we introduce to Christ.)*

v.37: *(Paul loved his friends deeply. We can ask God for a greater love for those whom we follow-up.)*

v.38: *(Paul's disciples responded to his godly love and concern. We will also be blessed through the response our disciples show to us as we carry out our ministry.)*

Say: Let us begin building our discipleship ministries by applying principles of Paul's ministry to our own. **One by one, write the following main points from Paul's example on your flip chart, and encourage students to take notes in**

their Study Guides. Give students time to answer each question and briefly discuss the answers for each point before going on to the next one.

1. Paul *identified* with the people to whom he ministered. He got involved in their lives.
   - How can you identify with those in your ministry?
2. Paul *imparted* truth. He did not shrink from teaching and preaching, but testified to the "whole will of God."
   - Why is it important to teach "all of God's Word"? What does this mean?
3. Paul *implanted* values and responsibilities. He explained not only what he was doing, but why he was doing it. Our disciples also need to know the why's and the how-to's of following Jesus.
   - What values and responsibilities do you want to teach new believers? Why are these important to know?
4. Paul's ministry *involved* personal sacrifice. Discipling cannot be done leisurely. It requires diligence and hard work.
   - What will it cost you to become a disciple-maker?

Say: During the last session, the Action Point emphasized sharing our faith in Christ. Now we want to learn how to motivate new believers we introduce to Christ to continue in their spiritual walk. To do that, we will discuss how to make appointments to begin follow-up.

Making a Follow-Up Appointment

This section of this lesson assumes that each student has introduced at least one person to Christ in the past few weeks. If one or two of your group members have not seen fruit in their witnessing, pair them with group members who have and continue with this lesson. Encourage these students individually after class.

If most of your students are still struggling with witnessing, complete this lesson. Then suspend the study and review witness training materials such as the *Reaching Your World Through Witnessing Without Fear* videos or the *Five Steps to Sharing Your Faith* Bible study. Take your students witnessing with you. When students are ready for follow-up, continue with Step 4.

Say: Some of you may feel uncertain about setting up that first appointment. To give us confidence, let us practice one way of making a follow-up appointment with a new believer.

Read the following steps for making a follow-up appointment, which are also in the Study Guide.

How to Make a Follow-Up Appointment

1. Seek an appointment to meet with new believers within 24 to 48 hours. It is important to meet with new Christians right away since they are so vulnerable to Satan's attacks.
2. Arrange a specific time and place convenient for both of you.
3. Encourage the new Christian to review the *Four Spiritual Laws* before you meet again. Then pray together, thanking the Lord Jesus once more for coming into your lives. Also encourage the person to read the first three chapters of John before the appointment. (If he does not have a Bible, offer to give him one.)

Using the Dialog Example at the end of this lesson, demonstrate with your partner how to encourage a new believer to attend a follow-up appointment.

After the demonstration, thank your partner, then discuss these questions:

- What did I say to start showing [partner's name] his need to grow in his walk with God?
- What did I do to set up the appointment?

Say: Building relationships is the foundation for helping new believers grow in their faith. Therefore, having and showing genuine love and concern is the most important ingredient in successful follow-up. Jesus did not just view His disciples as part of His goal to reach the world, they were also His closest friends. He was involved in their lives.

Keep the goal of building relationships foremost in your discipleship ministry. This will help you balance training with friendship. Too much emphasis on training will make new believers feel like a "ministry project." Friendship without training may result in new believers who are not growing spiritually and may cause your ministry to stray from its focus of disciplemaking. Instead, have fun and be serious. Plan lighthearted activities and share your vision for those who do not know Christ.

Also remember that we can make appointments with more mature Christians who are not involved in spiritual multiplication. During the appointments, we can challenge them to get involved in the discipleship process. One good way to do this is to invite them to a Bible study like this one. We will discuss that in greater detail later.

Now, let us practice setting up an appointment with a new believer.

Application (10 minutes)

As a group, read through the Dialog Example at the end of this lesson. This example applies to following up a new believer. When you finish, say: To make us feel more comfortable, let's use the Two-By-Two Practice method in setting up an appointment.

These are the directions for using the Two-By-Two Practice method for this lesson:

1. **Have students pick a partner, with one person taking the role of the discipler and the other taking the role of the new believer.**
2. **Allow three minutes for the first person to present the material. Have students exchange roles with**

their partners, then give them another three minutes to practice. Say: As you role-play, refer to the Dialog Example for help, but personalize the dialog.

3. **As pairs practice, walk around the room and listen to their presentations. Answer questions and give suggestions as needed.**
4. **After the practice session, ask students for their observations and questions.**

When the time is up, go through the Action Point in the Study Guide.

Closing and Prayer (2–5 minutes)

Say: During our next two sessions, we will discuss how to conduct a follow-up appointment and how to help new believers live Spirit-filled lives. This will help give us more confidence in our disciple-making ministry.

Thank God for giving you the privilege of being used in His work. Pray for opportunities for your members to witness and for their wisdom and courage in making follow-up appointments, especially the first one. Thank God for the power of His Holy Spirit that makes serving Him possible and enjoyable.

Remind your group to pray regularly for those with whom they are sharing.

Follow-Up

If you have students who have a hard time setting up appointments, practice with them individually and pray together for boldness. Give them tips from your experience on how to handle fears or feelings of inadequacy.

Student Lesson Plan

Basics of Follow-Up

Definition: Follow-up is the process by which new believers are established in the faith and equipped with the basics of Christianity so they can grow toward spiritual maturity and become multiplying disciples.

What part does each of the following principles play in the follow-up process?

1. Remember that God causes the spiritual growth (1 Corinthians 3:6,7; Philippians 1:6; 2:13).
2. Build relationships with new believers (Acts 2:41,42,46).
3. Motivate new believers to grow spiritually (2 Peter 3:18).
4. Introduce new believers to God's desire for all Christians to witness (Acts 1:8).
5. Encourage new Christians to become involved with other believers (Hebrews 10:24,25).
6. Pray regularly for those you follow-up (Colossians 4:12).
7. Meet regularly with new believers and teach them how to live Spirit-filled lives (Acts 11:25,26; Ephesians 5:18).
8. Challenge new believers and more mature Christians to become multiplying disciples (2 Timothy 2:2).

Purpose of follow-up: Christ sends us out to introduce others to Him, to help them become His disciples, and to teach them how to reach out to others (Matthew 28:18–20).

Paul's Example of Follow-Up

Write the four main points from Paul's example of follow-up, then answer the questions.

1\.

How can you identify with those in your ministry?

2.

Why is it important to teach "all of God's Word?" What does this mean?

3.

What values and responsibilities do you want to teach new believers? Why are these important to know?

4.

What will it cost you to become a disciple-maker?

Making a Follow-Up Appointment

How to Make a Follow-Up Appointment

1. Seek an appointment to meet with new believers within 24 to 48 hours. It is important to meet with new Christians right away since they are so vulnerable to Satan's attacks.
2. Arrange a specific time and place convenient for both of you.
3. Encourage the new Christian to review the *Four Spiritual Laws* before you meet again. Then pray together, thanking the Lord Jesus once more for coming into your lives. Also encourage the person to read the first three chapters of John before the appointment. (If he does not have a Bible, offer to give him one.)

Use the Dialog Example on the next page to practice making a follow-up appointment. Adapt it to your situation.

Action Point: Write the name of two or more new Christians or mature believers you will ask to set up an appointment. Then pray for your contact with each person. Before the next session, make a follow-up appointment with each person, but schedule these appointments after the next session because the lesson will cover how to conduct a follow-up appointment.

____

____

____

Dialog Example

Terry: Jack, when you invited Christ into your life today, you began a personal relationship with Him. But this is really only the beginning. You and I just met. In this sense we have begun a friendship, a personal relationship, too. But what if, after today, we never see or hear from each other again. Will our friendship grow?

Jack: No.

Terry: Why not?

Jack: Because a friendship depends on getting to know each other.

Terry: Right, and it's the same way with our Lord Jesus Christ. Even though you began a relationship with Him today, for you to grow, you need to know Him better. The better we know God, the more we can trust and obey Him. How do you think a friendship grows?

Jack: By spending time together, talking to each other and doing things together.

Terry: That's right. And we need to learn how to communicate with Christ and allow Him to communicate with us. That's why we spend time with Him. I'd like to get together with you again and share how you can build your friendship with God. Would you be interested?

Jack: Yes, I would.

Terry: Are you free next week at this time?

Jack: Yes.

Terry: Why don't we meet right here? Let's write that down.

Jack: Okay, that will be fine.

Terry: I encourage you to read through the *Four Spiritual Laws* again before we meet and thank Christ that He is in your life. By thanking God you demonstrate faith, and that pleases Him. You may also want to read the first three chapters of the Gospel of John before we meet.

I really enjoyed talking with you. I look forward to seeing you this time next week.

Inspire Others to Grow in Their Faith

Focus

A follow-up appointment helps meet two of the new believer's needs: 1) to gain assurance that Christ is living in him, and 2) to realize the value of participating in a Bible study group.

Objectives

This session will help students to:

- *Learn* how to conduct a follow-up appointment
- *Assure* new believers that Christ is living in them
- *Help* new believers begin their adventure with God
- *Encourage* new believers to join a Bible study group

Session Scripture

1 Peter 2:1–5

Outline

I. Topics for follow-up
II. Guidelines for follow-up
III. Conducting a follow-up appointment
IV. Closing a follow-up appointment

Leader's Preparation

This lesson has instructions for two follow-up practice sessions. If necessary, hold the number of sessions necessary for your students to feel confident about conducting follow-up appointments. If you are learning along with your students, be honest about your lack of experience and encourage everyone to participate in helping the group learn how to do follow-up. You may want to practice the follow-up procedures individually with students who feel inadequate or who have a difficult time building spiritual relationships.

The first follow-up appointment assures the new believer that he is a Christian; the second one helps new believers understand and practice Spirit-filled living through a process called Spiritual Breathing. The goal of both appointments is to get the new believer involved in a discipleship Bible study group. The first follow-up appointment is detailed in the lesson; the second one is outlined. Adapt the procedures from the first appointment to conduct the second one.

The first appointment uses the material from pages 11 through 15 of the *Four Spiritual Laws* booklet. The outline for the second follow-up appointment contains much of the same material as the booklet *Have You Made the Wonderful Discovery of the Spirit-Filled Life?* If your students are familiar with using a booklet such as the *Four Spiritual Laws*, they may prefer to use the *Spirit-Filled Life* booklet instead of following the outline.

Now that you know your students better, re-evaluate their commitments to discipleship. Review the chart from the Leader's Preparation in Step 1. If you have a student who does not appear to exhibit a "Heart for God" or is not developing a lifestyle of "Dependence on the Holy Spirit," you may want to privately help him review his commitment to God and discipleship.

The columns in this chart relate to a Christian's ongoing ministry of discipleship. If you see problems in these areas, you might consider asking the student to assist you in your discipleship ministry to further develop his discipleship and relational skills. You might also have a student join you in visitation or follow-up, and ask him to help you lead a discipleship Bible study. Working with reluctant students one-on-one may make the difference in their effectiveness as a disciple-maker.

This week, spend extra time in prayer for each of your students. Ask God to give them confidence, love, and boldness to become godly disciple-makers. In the remaining two sessions in this Bible study, help each person find the area of ministry that God gives him, compliment him for the strengths you see in his ministry, and encourage him to work on the weaknesses.

You may also want to encourage your students to read two of the Transferable Concepts, *How to Be Filled with the Holy Spirit* and *How to Walk in the Spirit*. These booklets will help them understand and apply the work of the Holy Spirit in their lives and ministry.

Before this session, practice demonstrating a follow-up appointment. Select a student to be your partner, and rehearse the demonstration until he knows which responses to make. Assume that your students know nothing about conducting follow-up appointments. Therefore, be specific and realistic in this demonstration, but keep your presentation simple. Your group members probably will closely imitate what you do.

Bring your flip chart and a copy of the *Four Spiritual Laws* for each person in the group.

The Bible Study Session

Sharing (5 minutes)

Ask members who attempted to make an initial follow-up appointment to share the results. Discuss any successes or problems they encountered.

Discussion Starter (8–10 minutes)

Point out the Sample Conversation at the end of the lesson in the Study Guide. Assure the students that you will show them how to use the dialog and give them a chance to practice conducting a follow-up appointment.

Then discuss: What do you think will be the hardest part of meeting with a new believer? **Use the information you receive from the answers to tailor the lesson around the needs of your group. For example, if several people**

express apprehension about starting a conversation about follow-up with a new believer, spend more of your class time on how to introduce the subject.

Lesson Development (15–20 minutes)

Topics for Follow-Up

Say: Just as a newborn baby needs food and loving attention soon after birth, a new believer needs spiritual food and fellowship right after his decision to follow Christ. **Read 1 Peter 2:1–5.** To help those we introduce to Christ begin growing spiritually, we will learn how to conduct follow-up appointments.

Read the Focus statement at the beginning of this lesson. Explain: The goals for follow-up are to:

- Help the new believer start growing in his faith.
- Give the new believer assurance of God's promises to all Christians.
- Encourage the new believer to get involved with other Christians through a Bible study group and join a Christ-honoring church.

At the end of this lesson, you will see directions for conducting two follow-up meetings with new believers. The most effective follow-up begins with individual meetings, then leads to involvement in a Bible study. The topics for the follow-up appointments are:

- How you can be sure you are a Christian
- How you can experience Spirit-filled living

The follow-up appointments will also help you begin to build leadership skills for guiding a Bible study group. During the next two sessions, you will begin planning for your own group. You may want to team up with one or two other group members to start and lead this group.

Now let us look at the guidelines for conducting follow-up appointments.

Guidelines for Follow-Up

Ask students to turn to this section in their Study Guides. Give them a few moments to read the five guidelines, then discuss how each contributes to the follow-up appointment.

1. *Have a clear objective for each appointment.* Keeping the objective in mind will help you stay on the subject.
2. *Establish rapport with the new Christian.* It is important to establish rapport during the first few minutes of the appointment. Be enthusiastic, be friendly, and seek to create a desire in the new believer to grow in Christ. Ask how things have gone since you last met.
3. *Ask if he has read the material you gave him at your last meeting.* Help him with any questions he might have.
4. *Go through the follow-up material.* For example, during the first appointment, review the *Four Spiritual Laws.*
5. *Be relaxed but attentive to the person's needs.* Watch the time, and if the person has other obligations to keep, cut the time short. On the other hand, do not hurry away if the new believer wants to talk about personal issues. He may be more open to talking now than he was before.

Say: Here are some points to remember when closing the follow-up appointment:

- *Let him know that you enjoyed your time together,* and that you would like to meet again to talk more about God and the Christian life.
- *Encourage him to join your Bible study group.* Tell him the time and place, and offer to give him a ride if he feels hesitant. Personal follow-up is a bridge to group follow-up. It is important to involve new believers with other Christians as soon as possible, because without the support of other Christians, few new believers grow to spiritual maturity.
- *Invite him to attend church* with you or recommend a Christ-honoring church in his area.

- *Invite him to go witnessing with you.* Witnessing is an important tool for discipleship, and new believers should be encouraged to participate as soon as they are ready.
- *Close your appointment in prayer.*

Say: Now let's learn how to conduct a follow-up appointment.

Conducting a Follow-Up Appointment

Say: It is important to help new Christians be sure that Christ lives in them. People who are sure of their salvation are secure in their relationship with God. Only God brings assurance of salvation, but you can help a new believer trust in the promises of God's Word.

When you meet, begin with the assurance section on page 11 of the *Four Spiritual Laws*. **Distribute copies of the *Four Spiritual Laws* to the students and ask them to turn to page 11.** Read the material and ask the questions. Listen to the new Christian's answers, and evaluate and clarify them until he understands Christ's indwelling presence. Your objective is not just to cover the content, but also to make sure the new believer grasps the biblical principle of the assurance of salvation. The following procedures for using the *Four Spiritual Laws* will help make the follow-up appointment more interesting for the new believer. There is a place to write them in your Study Guides. **Write these procedures on your flip chart:**

1. Look up the verses in your Bible.
2. Ask the new Christian to read the verses.
3. Read the question.
4. Invite the new Christian to answer the question. Discuss it if appropriate, and restate the answer correctly if necessary.

Ask your partner to come forward to help demonstrate the follow-up appointment. Have students observe as you use the principles and methods, and ask them to take notes in their Study Guides. Invite them to look up the Bible references along with you and your partner.

To begin the demonstration, say: Assume that the new believer and I have spent several minutes talking, building a friendship. **Give the demonstration, using the Sample Conversation as a guideline. Stop at the bracketed instruction, "Finish the rest of the booklet in the same manner."**

Ask if the students have any questions on your demonstration, then have them form pairs to do a Two-By-Two Practice of the appointment. To begin the practice session, say: We will practice conducting an appointment by using the Two-By-Two Practice method. **Review the practice method. Then say:** Follow the Sample Conversation, stopping at the instruction: "Finish the rest of the booklet in the same manner." All this material comes from the *Four Spiritual Laws* booklet. Then continue using the *Four Spiritual Laws* until you reach the end of the booklet. Start now.

After three minutes, ask partners to switch roles. Give students another three minutes to practice, then discuss any questions or comments they have.

Closing a Follow-Up Appointment

Say: The next section of the Sample Conversation shows you how to close the appointment. The Sample Conversation gives two invitations. The first one invites the new believer to a Bible study group to help him grow spiritually. This is a very important step for the new believer to assure that he continues in his faith. If he does not join a Bible study at this time, invite him to continue meeting with you one-on-one so you can personally encourage his Christian growth until he is ready to join a group. For some new believers, it take a little transition time before they feel comfortable joining a study group.

The second invitation will help the new believer begin sharing his faith right away. Your witnessing can be a learning tool for him and can help him experience the joy of introducing others to Jesus Christ. As you bring him alongside as you witness, he will begin to become a multiplying disciple.

Using Two-By-Two Practice, have students finish practicing the Sample Conversation. Then say: This lesson includes an outline for a second follow-up appointment because some new Christians may not be ready to join a Bible study group. Or perhaps your group will not begin meeting for a couple of weeks. It is essential for a new Christian's spiritual growth that he have continuing contact with other believers.

Say: If you want to learn more about conducting follow-up, we can meet for one extra week. If we agree to add another week to our Bible study sessions, next week we'll practice the second appointment instead of going on to the next Step. This will help us all feel more comfortable about conducting appointments. **See if your students want to meet once more, then schedule the time and place.**

Application (8 minutes)

Go over the Evaluation and Action Point in the Study Guide. Discuss your students' plans to conduct follow-up appointments and offer to help them if necessary.

Closing and Prayer (2–3 minutes)

Pray for opportunities to witness and ask for God's guidance as your group does follow-up. Be specific about praying for your students' concerns as they contact new believers. Encourage them to make appointments even if they are apprehensive. Remind them that they also need to be planning a Bible study group so they can invite new believers to attend.

Follow-Up

Write down the names of the new believers to be contacted and pray for them during the week. Encourage your students by telephone or in person as they make their appointments and do follow-up. If necessary, go along with the students who lack confidence in their ability to do follow-up.

Student Lesson Plan

Guidelines for Follow-Up

How do you think each of these guidelines contributes to the follow-up appointment?

1. *Have a clear objective for each appointment.* Keeping the objective in mind will help you stay on the subject.
2. *Establish rapport with the new Christian.* It is important to establish rapport during the first few minutes of the appointment. Be enthusiastic, be friendly, and seek to create in the new believer a desire to grow in Christ. Ask how things have gone since you last met.
3. *Ask if he has read the material you gave him at your last meeting.* Help him with any questions he might have.
4. *Go through the follow-up material.* For example, during the first appointment, review the *Four Spiritual Laws.*
5. *Be relaxed but attentive to the person's needs.* Watch the time, and if the person has other obligations to keep, cut the time short. On the other hand, do not hurry away if the new believer wants to talk about personal issues. He may be more open to talking now than he was before.

Follow these guidelines when closing your appointment:

- *Let him know that you enjoyed your time together,* and that you would like to meet again to talk more about God and the Christian life.
- *Encourage him to join your Bible study group.* Tell him the time and place, and offer to give him a ride if he feels hesitant. Personal follow-up is a bridge to group follow-up. It is important to involve new believers with other Christians as soon as possible, because without the support of other Christians, few new believers grow to spiritual maturity.
- *Invite him to attend church* with you or recommend a Christ-honoring church in his area.

- *Invite him to go witnessing with you.* Witnessing is an important tool for discipleship, and new believers should be encouraged to participate as soon as they are ready.
- *Close your appointment in prayer.*

Conducting a Follow-Up Appointment

Record the procedures for using the *Four Spiritual Laws* follow-up material:

1.
2.
3.
4.

Observing the procedures used in conducting a follow-up appointment will be very helpful to you as you prepare for your own appointments. Write your observations of the class demonstration here:

Evaluation: Evaluating your personal rehearsal is valuable to you. Write your observations of your practice session here:

What improvements would you like to make in your presentation?

Action Point: Apply what you have learned in these lessons with the people you are currently following up. Record how you plan to use this information in your personal ministry:

Use the space below to list those you contact for follow-up appointments and to describe the results. Keep track of times and dates and how the appointments went. Remember: your goal is to get new believers involved in a Bible study group.

Sample Conversation for the First Follow-Up Appointment

The following Sample Conversation should be used as a guideline for conducting a follow-up appointment. Do not use it word for word. Instead, communicate the content in a natural way. Remember, the Lord is concerned with people, not methods. His Holy Spirit does the work through us—the methods just help us to be more efficient.

Terry: Jack, I'm glad we're able to get together again. Have you thought any more about our discussion yesterday?

Jack: Yes, I have. But I'm still trying to understand what all this will mean in my life.

Terry: I can identify with that. As I mentioned yesterday, when you invited Christ into your life, you began a new relationship. It takes time to get to know Him. I had the same thoughts you have and that's why I'm excited about getting together with you and explaining some of these things to you. I had a friend who did that with me and it really helped. Did you have a chance to review the Four Spiritual Laws and thank God for coming into your life?

Jack: Yes, but I fell asleep before I could read any of the Gospel of John.

Terry: I understand. I sometimes have trouble staying awake at night too. I want to encourage you to begin reading through that Gospel. It will give you a clear picture of who Christ is. Do you have any questions about the things we talked about yesterday?

Jack: Not right now.

Terry: Okay, then let's review the part in the *Four Spiritual Laws* on how we can know Christ is in our life. Let's look at the questions together.

[Turn to page 11 in your *Four Spiritual Laws* booklet.]

Terry: I'll read the questions and look up the verse in my Bible. Then we'll discuss them.

Jack: That sounds good.

Terry: The first questions is: Did you receive Christ into your life?

Jack: Yes.

Terry: According to His promise in Revelation 3:20, where is Jesus Christ right now in relation to you?

Jack: In my heart.

Terry: That's right. Christ said that he would come into your life. Would He mislead you?

Jack: No.

Terry: On what authority do you know that God has answered your prayer when you invited Christ into your life?

Jack: He said He would come in.

Terry: That's right. Our faith is in the trustworthiness of God and His Word.

[Finish the rest of the booklet in the same manner.]

Terry: Well, Jack, I enjoyed going through this booklet with you. I hope it was helpful.

Jack: Yes, it really was. I didn't realize God gave us so many promises in the Bible.

Terry: Right after I received Christ, it helped to have my friend show me additional truths about God and answer my questions. I am going to join [or lead] a Bible study group that will help Christians grow spiritually. Are you interested in participating in a group like that?

Jack: Yes, but what would be involved?

Terry: The Bible study group will meet once a week for an hour. In this group, you can bring up any questions you might have about your new life in Christ and you will get to know other Christians.

Jack: That sounds really interesting to me.

Terry: Great. It begins on Tuesday at 8 o'clock. Is that good for you?

Jack: Yes, that would be fine.

Terry: I'll call you on Monday to remind you. Would you like me to pick you up?

Jack: That's a good idea.

Terry: I am so excited about what God is doing. In fact, I really enjoy talking with others about my faith in Christ. Would you like to go with me as I explain to someone else about Christ like I did with you yesterday?

Jack: Well, I'm not sure I'm ready for that. Would I have to say anything?

Terry: No. you can just listen. I'd really enjoy the company. Would Saturday afternoon be good for you?

Jack: Sure, I could make that.

Terry: Good. I'll come by and pick you up around 1:30.

Jack: Thanks. I'll be waiting. See you then.

[In the next few weeks, invite the new Christian to attend church with you and spend time together in a social setting. For instance, you could invite him to join you for lunch after church.]

Outline for the Second Follow-Up Appointment

Objective: To help the new believer understand and practice Spirit-filled living.

1. Read Romans 8:35–39. Discuss how permanent God's love is.
2. Read John 10:10. Discuss how God wants us to have an exciting, abundant life. Ask, "Why do many Christians fail to experience this abundant life?" *(Because they do not surrender every part of their life to God or have unconfessed sin in their life.)*
3. Read Romans 8:5–8. Explain how unconfessed sin short-circuits the flow of God's power. Say, "Confessing sin immediately keeps your relationship with God vital and growing."
4. Ask, "If Christ has already paid the penalty for our sins, why should we confess them?" *(Christ has forgiven us once and for all. By confessing our sins, we show that we agree that our action is wrong in God's eyes and that we understand what God has done for us through Jesus.)*
5. Ask, "Does God stop loving us when we sin?" *(No.)*
6. Say, "We can stop being worldly and sinful and experience God's love and forgiveness by practicing Spiritual Breathing. Describe the process of physical breathing: we breathe in pure air and exhale impure air. Compare what happens to your body if you stop breathing with what happens to your spiritual life if you do not confess sin. Emphasize that you cannot lose your spiritual life, but you can become useless to God if you are bound in sin.
7. Read 1 John 1:9 and explain exhaling—confessing our sin.
8. Read Ephesians 5:18 and explain inhaling—appropriating the power of the Holy Spirit as an act of our will by faith.

9. Lead the new believer in Spiritual Breathing:

   Exhale:

   Ask the Holy Spirit to bring to your mind any unconfessed sin.

   Confess your sin and claim the promise of 1 John 1:9.

   Make restitution for the sin if necessary.

   Inhale:

   Claim the filling of the Spirit by faith as commanded in Ephesians 5:18 and promised in 1 John 5:14,15.

10. Encourage the new believer to start a habit of daily Bible reading. Read aloud Psalm 119:97–100 and 1 Peter 2:2. Explain how God's Word is food for our new life in Christ. Encourage him to begin by reading one chapter of the New Testament each day, beginning with the Gospel of John.

11. Emphasize that memorizing Scripture is an excellent way to make God's Word a part of his life. Write John 3:16; 1 John 1:9; Matthew 28:18–20; Ephesians 2:8,9; and Romans 8:1,2 on a slip of paper or a card. Give it to him and ask him to memorize one verse each day, reviewing each he has learned every day.

12. Explain to the new believer how to have a quiet time with God.

13. Encourage the new believer again to learn more about his new life in Christ by joining a Bible study group.

14. If the new believer is still hesitant about joining a Bible study group or your group is not yet meeting, arrange to meet again. Together, go over 2 Timothy 3:16,17; Philippians 4:6,7; Hebrews 10:24,25; and John 14:21.

15. Pray together, thanking God for His love and forgiveness.

[Encourage your disciple to read the Transferable Concept, *How to Love by Faith*. Obtain the booklet at a Christian bookseller or call New*Life* Publications at (800) 235-7255 to order.]

Prepare to Lead a Discipleship Group

Focus

An effective discipleship group leader keeps his objective in mind and applies the elements of spiritual multiplication to motivate and equip new believers to multiply spiritually.

Objectives

This session will help students to:

- *Discover* the role of a leader
- *Study* the elements of a healthy small group
- *Begin selecting* disciples for their own group
- *Prepare* for the first meeting of their discipleship group

Session Scriptures

Matthew 24:14; 28:18–20; John 13:34; 14:1; Romans 12:3–8; 15:2,14–18; 1 Corinthians 3:5–9; Galatians 6:1,2; 1 Thessalonians 5:24; 1 John 3:17

Outline

I. The Discipleship Process
II. Your Leadership Role
III. The Role of a Discipleship Group
  A. A Plan to Evangelize
  B. An Environment for Growth
IV. Selecting Disciples
V. The Final Challenge
VI. Leading the First Meeting

Leader's Preparation

A small group is the best means for building spiritual multipliers and reaching people with God's message of love and forgiveness. This lesson will help you challenge your disciples to lead their own groups.

This lesson also encourages members to develop a plan for evangelism. Before the session begins, select several evangelism tools that you can present to your group. You might bring a copy of the *"JESUS"* video; *A Man Without Equal* video or book; the *Four Spiritual Laws*; *The Joy of Hospitality*, which presents a home-based method of evangelism; the *Five Steps of Christian Growth*, a Bible study that includes evangelistic lessons; the booklets *Jesus and the Intellectual* and *A Great Adventure*; or other materials that you have used. Familiarize yourself with how to use the tools that you bring to the session.

Also, fill out the Leadership Questionnaire in the Student Lesson Plan. Think through how you will describe your commitment to keeping a balanced schedule so you can present your ideas to the group.

During the Application of this lesson, your students will roleplay the first few minutes of a group meeting. You can also roleplay additional parts of the meeting to allow group members to take turns leading the lesson, although this will take more time than allotted for the lesson. If you decide to conduct a sample meeting, call your group members before the session and plan to meet for an extra half hour or so.

Bring your flip chart to this session.

The Bible Study Session

Sharing (5 minutes)

Ask volunteers to share what happened during their follow-up appointments. Also ask them to describe how they could better meet the new believer's needs in a future appointment. Encourage students who have not yet met with new Christians to do so.

Discussion Starter (5 minutes)

Talk about Bible study groups that you or your students have attended in the past. Identify qualities in small groups that are helpful to spiritual growth. Discuss pitfalls of leading a group and characteristics of good small group leadership. As you discuss, be careful not to have a critical spirit toward other Bible study leaders.

Lesson Development (25–30 minutes)

The Discipleship Process

Say: Now that we have reached the final session in our Bible study, we will begin putting all the pieces of our discipleship ministry together. Let me read a story about someone who was led through the discipleship process, so you can see how all the parts fit into the whole. **Read:**

> One day, a pre-med student named Lee saw a young man sitting alone on the University of California, San Diego, campus. Lee was involved in a discipleship group that reached out to non-Christian students, so he introduced himself. Lee learned that Imad was a pre-med student who had just transferred from another university. Imad was a Palestinian from Jordan.
>
> Lee asked Imad if he would agree to be part of a religious survey. Imad agreed, but only because Lee seemed like such a kind person. After the survey was completed, they talked about other topics for a few minutes. Then Lee shared the *Four Spiritual Laws* with his new friend. Imad did not understand completely why he needed to receive Christ as his Savior, but he did consent to attend the Bible study Lee was leading.
>
> When Imad joined the group, he met other people whom Lee and his Christian friends had contacted. After six weeks of attending, Imad became convicted of his sin and realized his need for a Savior. He received Christ through prayer during a Friday night meeting on campus. Immediately, he sensed a real joy and the presence of Christ in his life. He had a deep hunger to read God's holy Word.

Lee encouraged Imad to join a Bible study group for Christian growth. Through the study, Imad learned how to have a daily quiet time with God, study God's Word, and pray. Lee also began to take Imad with him as he shared the gospel with others. First Imad just watched, then he read through the *Four Spiritual Laws* with unbelievers while Lee watched. Soon Imad was going out witnessing on his own.

Lee challenged Imad to begin his own Bible study group. By the time Imad graduated two years later, he had trained a spiritual generation of believers who were leading their own Bible studies and who had trained another spiritual generation of new believers to witness and lead their own Bible studies.

After graduation, Imad realized that going on to medical school was not what God wanted him to do. Although he was accepted into a prestigious medical university, he returned to Jordan to help reach Arabs with the gospel. He received a doctorate in theology and is now president of the Jordan Evangelical Theology Seminary in Amman, Jordan. JETS trains Arabic-speaking people from the Middle East and northern Africa to return to their homes and win Muslims to Christ.

Because of Lee's faithfulness in spiritual multiplication and discipleship, his influence is now having a worldwide impact! Because of Imad's faithfulness to God's call for discipleship, he is touching a part of the world that most others cannot reach!

Ask:

- What helped Imad grow so quickly in his faith? *(He had a hunger for God; Lee was faithful in discipling him; he got involved with other Christians right away.)*
- How does the story illustrate the principle of spiritual multiplication? *(Because of Lee's investment in Imad's life, Imad has reached many people for our Lord whom Lee could never been able to reach and trained them to multiply spiritually.)*
- What were the Win, Build, Train, Send steps in this story? *(Win—Lee witnessed to Imad; build—Imad joined Lee's Bible study; Train—Lee discipled Imad both one-on-one and in a group setting; Send—Imad began his own Bible studies with his new converts.)*

Say: That is an inspiring example of what can happen in each of our ministries under the power of the Holy Spirit. Let's begin by reviewing what a discipleship ministry is, then look at the role of a leader within that context.

Your Leadership Role

Say: A discipleship Bible study is not an end in itself. It is a tool to help us reach our corner of the world for Christ. Let us read the Great Commission once again to review the task our Savior has given us. **Read Matthew 28:18–20.**

Say: We are to teach other Christians to be spiritual multipliers. The Great Commission includes teaching believers *to obey* all that Christ commands us. More than just providing knowledge about God's Word, it means creating an atmosphere that encourages people to apply godly principles in their lives.

The Great Commission also includes the command to *make disciples of all nations.* Making disciples means equipping believers not only to witness, but also to train other new believers to become spiritual multipliers.

Creating an environment that encourages spiritual growth is a part of your job as a leader. Let us look at some principles of good leadership that can help you build a core group. These principles are given in your Study Guides. **Read each paragraph and the verses, then discuss the question.**

1. *A good leader builds an atmosphere of trusting God* (John 14:1). Our Lord must be the focus of our study groups. We do not merely study about God, we get to know Him personally and learn to trust Him with every area of our life and ministry. **Ask:**

   - Why is sharing specific areas of your life in which you are trusting God so essential to your leadership role?

2. *A good leader encourages a mindset of ministering to others* (Romans 15:2; 1 John 3:17). We do not want to become ingrown (considering only our own interests), but rather reach out to others to meet their needs. **Ask:**

- As a leader, how can you help group members evaluate how much time they are spending in ministry to others?

3. *A good leader cultivates an attitude of loving relationships* (John 13:34). Many factors can cause people to join a group, but only loving, Christ-centered relationships will keep them involved. **Ask:**

- What kinds of things can a leader do to help develop loving relationships among group members?

4. *A good leader creates a vision for reaching his community and the world* (Matthew 24:14). Acquiring a vision does not happen by itself; the leader must help the vision develop. Help students find a vision for helping to fulfill the Great Commission by praying together for your community and the world and by sharing witnessing experiences. **Ask:**

- How has sharing witnessing experiences helped your vision for reaching others?

5. *A good leader provides loving accountability for group members* (Galatians 6:1,2). Greater spiritual growth results when Christians encourage each other to do the right thing. Here are ways you can help group members be accountable:

   a. *Get involved in their lives.* Do not just meet once a week, but get involved in the day-to-day lives of others and encourage them to do the same.

   b. *Help members apply God's holy Word to their lives.* Study the Bible with them, then model how to live the principles. Help them apply what they are learning to specific areas of their lives. Encourage them to set spiritual goals and pray with them about achieving these goals.

   c. *Minister together.* Practical application is essential to learning. Imagine a doctor learning how to do surgery from a book! To help members, walk alongside them as they develop the necessary skills to witness, conduct follow-up appointments, and lead a group. Then hold them accountable for using their skills.

Say: A leader will not achieve his goals if he is too tired or feels overwhelmed by his task. Our ministry should be an overflow of our intimate walk with Jesus. An effective leader disciplines himself to give time to his family, church, and job as well as his ministry. He also takes time for personal needs and fun.

Does this seem impossible? The key is to evaluate your schedule and plan for daily needs and ministry. Otherwise, either your ministry or your daily responsibilities will take too much time. Also, evaluating your schedule will help you find creative ways to manage all you want to do.

For example, you might consider hosting evangelistic events in your home and involving your family members. Or perhaps you could lead a discipleship Bible study with new Christians at your job during your lunch hour. And do not be afraid of asking group members to shoulder some of the responsibilities, such as planning refreshments or opening their homes for meetings. As they are trained, give them more responsibilities, such as acting as prayer coordinator, contacting other members between sessions, or even encouraging partners go witnessing together.

To help you keep your ministry balanced, fill out the Leadership Questionnaire in the Study Guide. **Give students a few moments to fill out the questionnaire, then allow volunteers to describe what they have planned. Also, share how you manage your schedule.**

Say: Now let us look at the role a small group plays in the discipleship process and how small groups can be effectively used for greater spiritual growth.

The Role of a Discipleship Group

Say: I am sure most of you have attended Bible studies that were content-oriented where you discussed what the Bible says. Perhaps you were challenged to apply what you learned, but for the most part, you just learned facts and ideas.

A discipleship Bible study emphasizes active ministry. Bible knowledge is important in this process, but application is just as essential. Let us consider what a discipleship group is not.

1. *It is not just a discussion group.* It has a strategy to Win, Build, Train, and Send new Christians into all the world.
2. *The goal is not merely to add people to the group.* The goal is to produce spiritual multipliers.
3. *It is not just a fellowship meeting.* Although fellowship is a vital element, a discipleship group is a place for prayer, Bible study, training, and vision.
4. *It is not just for evangelistic outreach.* The focus is to train others to do evangelism, not just witness as a group. Also, a group helps believers grow in all areas of the Christian life. A discipleship group provides an environment in which practical application of biblical truth takes place during a ministry of evangelism and discipleship.

Say: In addition to having a plan to evangelize, a healthy discipleship group creates an environment that encourages others to use their abilities and develop relationships with each other.

A Plan to Evangelize

Say: Many Christians have a desire to reach people with God's message of love and forgiveness, but they do not know how to begin. They may talk to a neighbor or friend about Christ, but are not very effective in their witness. As a group leader, you can help your members become more fruitful. To do this, you can offer evangelism tools that will help them reach more people and encourage them to have a plan to reach people with whom they have the most opportunity and influence.

Discuss how to use the evangelism tools you brought to class and identify the target group for each tool. For example, *The Joy of Hospitality* can be used in a neighborhood or home ministry, the *Four Spiritual Laws* are effective with one-on-one evangelism, the "*JESUS*" video or *A Man Without Equal* video can be used with larger groups. The booklets *Jesus and the Intellectual* and *A Great Adventure* can be handed to individuals.

Say: It is important to have a plan for evangelism and to target a group of people whom you want to reach. That way, you can plan events and schedule time to contact these people.

You may want to suggest an event that your group can organize or identify a group of people whom you could target. For example, you could plan neighborhood evangelism with the goal of beginning neighborhood Bible studies. Or you may want to plan your discipleship ministry around your church outreach program. Encourage members to outline their plans in their Study Guides.

An Environment for Growth

Say: No one leader can supply a complete environment for spiritual growth. Nor can one person supply all that another Christian needs for personal growth. We must help our disciples become active members of the body of Christ, not just a part of our ministry group. As a leader, you can help your group members get acquainted with other believers who will contribute to their growth and development. This is especially useful for areas in which you are less gifted or experienced.

Form two groups. Ask each group to read Romans 12:3–8 and 1 Corinthians 3:5–9, and discuss the three questions. Have groups report their answers to the class.

- What might happen if students are limited to one person's leadership for an extended period of time? *(They may become dependent on that leader; they will not be as well-rounded in their faith; they may not be challenged to use all their abilities; they may stifle God's leading in their lives.)*
- What are some ways we are connected to other ministries? *(For example, members may be involved in a men's or women's ministry, church outreach program, ministry to the homeless, and so on. Emphasize the importance of being actively involved in a local church.)*
- How can being a part of a church and of other ministries contribute to members' growth? *(They will gain a larger vision for what God is doing; they can receive help in areas*

not addressed by the group; they will have fellowship after the small group has disbanded.)

Say: Discipleship is an exciting ministry for many reasons. Lively interaction with a variety of people and growing interpersonal relationships provide an enriching experience. Let us look at the main elements of a healthy group environment. **Invite students to take notes in this section of their Study Guides as you discuss the points.**

1. *Sharing.* Relationships are central in a small group. A time of sharing helps people see how God is working in the lives of other growing Christians. It also allows students to see that everyone struggles with some areas in their lives and ministries. At first, members may not share openly. But as you develop a loving atmosphere and set an example by sharing yourself, they will respond more and more. **Ask:**
    - In your opinion, why is a sharing time important for connecting with each other?
2. *Prayer and praise time.* Opening the meeting in prayer helps people focus on God. Closing in prayer will allow you to pray for each other and thank and praise God for what He is doing in your group. **Ask:**
    - How has prayer helped you during our study times?
3. *Discussion.* This helps group members think through the biblical truths presented and leads to personal application. During the meeting, discuss how you can apply the study principles to daily life. Remember that the goal is not to cover content only, but to deal with real-life issues. **Ask:**
    - In your opinion, what are the pitfalls of a discussion time? How can a leader help eliminate them?
4. *Building a vision.* Unless our faith is stretched, most of us will be content to stay the same. A small group should expose members to what God is doing locally and around the world, challenging them to be a part of ministry. **Ask:**

- How has your vision changed as a result of attending this group?

5. *Training.* As we have discussed, a small group should equip members for a ministry of spiritual multiplication. **Ask:**
   - How has this training helped you in your witnessing?
6. *One-on-one help.* Individual training helps to personalize biblical truths and ministry skills. Class time is only one part of the training. To be truly life-changing, the training must be built into the student's life until it is applied, and sometimes this is best done on an individual basis. **Ask:**
   - What might happen to individual spiritual growth without one-on-one training outside of class time?
7. *Personal relationships.* Relationships need to be built on more than a spiritual level. Although that is the basis on which good friendships are developed, members should also enjoy fun times together. This helps keep relationships balanced in many ways. **Ask:**
   - What has been the most enjoyable for you during the weeks our group has met?

Selecting Disciples

Say: Not everyone you introduce to Christ and disciple will go on to be a spiritual multiplier. Just as in the parable of the sower (Mark 4:3–20) that we read earlier, some people will seem enthusiastic about Christ, but will soon fall away. Others will multiply themselves many times.

From among His followers Jesus selected disciples whom He provided more in-depth training. He took them with Him as He reached others (John 4; 6), He taught them from the Scriptures (Luke 24:36–49), and He sent them out to witness (Luke 10). We can follow His example. The first step is to select people who will follow Christ with their whole heart. Remember, however, not everyone you choose will be faithful to the calling. Judas was one of the twelve disciples, yet he betrayed Jesus. Let us look at the qualities of a potential disciple.

Ask group members to turn to this section in their Study Guides. Read through the following points and questions. Give students a few minutes to answer the questions about a new Christian they want to ask to join their group.

1. *A heart for God:* Does the person have a deep commitment to seek God? Here are some ways to tell: What does he talk about? Does his conversation tend to center around the Lord? Do his decisions glorify God?
2. *Dependence on the Holy Spirit:* Does the person demonstrate the fruit of the Spirit (Galatians 5:22,23) in daily life? Does he demonstrate faith in tough circumstances? How does he respond when things do not go well?
3. *Teachability:* Does this person ask questions about God's Word and ministry?
4. *Ability to build relationships:* Does the person have close friends? Do people like to be around him? Does he like to be around people? Does he give of himself to others?
5. *Relational thinking* (relating all areas of life to an ultimate purpose of glorifying God): Does this person have the purpose in life to glorify God? Does he relate decisions to this purpose and organize life's details around this purpose?
6. *Availability:* God is not looking for people with exceptional ability, but those who will be available for His work. Will this person make time for witnessing and being part of a Bible study? Does he follow through with his commitments or does he begin a task to abandon it when something more "exciting" comes along?

Say: It is important to look for these qualities in the Christians we disciple. No one can have all these qualities to a great degree, but the person who is growing in these areas will likely become a good disciple-maker.

Perhaps you are wondering just how to challenge those you select to join your discipleship group. After you have completed your follow-up appointments, have seen this person grow in his faith, and have decided that he might be a good member of your group, follow this plan:

1. Ask God if He is leading you to work with this person.
2. Meet with this person individually and share your vision for fulfilling the biblical call to spiritual multiplication. Be specific about how God can use a small group in these ways:
   - To help him in his spiritual growth and ministry
   - To contribute to his fellowship and relationships
   - To provide personal training in how to share his faith
3. Explain what is required of a member in your discipleship group: to model godly living in your Christian life, a commitment of time, and witnessing as a lifestyle.
4. Give him a few days to think over his decision. Tell him that you will be praying for him, and that you will check with him on a certain date to find out his answer. Assure him that a "no" answer will not change your relationship.

Say: I would like to challenge you to give yourself wholeheartedly to the task of making disciples. It is the most rewarding ministry any person could have. Let us look at how we can meet that challenge.

The Final Challenge

Say: Perhaps you are afraid that you will not have the ability to make disciples. Since God is the one who calls us to make disciples for Jesus Christ, He will enable us to complete the task. **Read 1 Thessalonians 5:24.** But some of you may still feel hesitant. Let me read to you what Paul says about our work. **Read Romans 15:14–16.**

Say: Paul had confidence that his disciples—and disciples through the centuries—would faithfully help fulfill the Great Commission. I am convinced that you, too, will follow through with our training. Paul goes on to say: **Read Romans 15:17,18.**

Continue: That is all God asks of us. To speak of Christ and what He has done for us, and thereby lead people to the Savior and teach them to obey God. And He has not left us on our own to accomplish this task. He gives us all that we need to serve Him. Do you remember these points as we studied them earlier?

Write the following points on your flip chart as you give them. Say: God has given us:

- *Authority and power*—God calls us to *minister* in the authority and power of Jesus.
- *Imperative*—God commands us to *make disciples* because that is His strategy for reaching the world.
- *Scope*—God desires that the entire *world* hear about Jesus.
- *Task*—As Jesus' disciples, we are called to a ministry of both *evangelism* and *discipleship*.
- *Expectation*—We can be sure that our *hard work* in the power of the Holy Spirit will be *blessed* by God.

Say: A discipleship ministry is a process that will take many weeks to complete. It needs to be tailored to your situation and to the people with whom you are working.

You cannot Win, Build, Train, and Send all at the same time. Let us review the chart "Process for Building Multiplying Disciples" in Step 2.

We should always be actively involved in Part 1, evangelism. Follow-up appointments will serve as intermediate training in Part 2. The *Five Steps of Christian Growth* Bible study is an effective method of helping new believers who need basic training in Christian living or for those who are not yet believers but want to know more about the Christian life.

In Part 3, we teach new Christians how to share their faith. This step should be encouraged right after the person becomes a Christian. The best method is to take new Christians along with you as you witness. We can also give advanced training through a Bible study called *Five Steps to Sharing Your Faith*.

Part 4, of course, is training new Christians (and older ones too) in disciple-making just like we are doing in our group. This is the leadership training part of the process.

I encourage you to be involved in all parts of this process. However, another effective way to accomplish our goal is to cooperate with each other. All of us should be winning people to Christ as a way of life, and should personally follow-up those whom we introduce to Christ. But we could divide up the other parts of the training. Perhaps one person will be directed by God to lead an intermediate Bible study, another an advanced training, or someone else the leadership training.

Now, to let you get the feel for leading a group, let us role-play a first group meeting.

Application (20 minutes)

Leading the First Meeting

Say: The purpose of your first discipleship group meeting is to start developing relationships within the group and to determine the commitment each person has made to discipleship. This is how to begin your first meeting:

1. Help group members get to know one another. Ask them to share their personal testimonies or what God is doing in their lives.
2. Explain your vision of what God will do in the group. Be enthusiastic.
3. Review the commitment they have made to discipleship and the benefits of being involved in a discipleship group.
4. Then begin with your Bible study lesson.

Say: As a group leader, you have your strengths and weaknesses. In leading your group, you will be able to identify what is easy for you to do and what is difficult. But we can learn a few practical tips that will help us avoid some of the common pitfalls of leading a group. These are listed in your Study Guides.

- *Losing sight of your objective.* Remember that your objective is to build spiritual multipliers, not just lead a Bible study group.
- *Lack of ministry with group members.* Your group will not begin to multiply spiritually unless you and your students develop a lifestyle of evangelism, follow-up, and discipleship. Much of this must take place outside the group meetings.
- *Lack of prayer.* Only the Holy Spirit can enable you and your students to multiply spiritually. A lack of prayer indicates a lack of dependence on God. Schedule time for prayer, so you will not put it off.
- *Weak selection of group members.* The temptation a leader faces is to allow people to be part of your group who are not faithful, available, and teachable. It is much better to train one person who goes on to train others than to have ten or fifteen people who never apply the principles.
- *Little personal involvement with members.* If you meet only during group time and an occasional ministry appointment, you will not be able to help them apply the principles of spiritual growth in their lifestyle. Plan social times too.
- *Leading a poor discussion time.* Leading a discussion is an art. As you become more experienced, you will find methods of discussion that fit your leadership style. Until then, remember these tips:

  Poor preparation can stifle discussion. Good preparation helps students get the greatest benefit from the lesson questions.

  Dominating leadership quenches discovery. Allowing everyone to share, ask questions, and express opinions or needs helps you better understand your group's strengths and weaknesses. It also makes members feel more valued.

  Asking ineffective questions, such as ones with yes and no answers, limits discussion. Good questions will help students think deeply and apply the principles to their lives.

Little or no application will keep the discussion from becoming profitable. Pointing out the biblical principles and relating them to everyday life will help produce life changes.

- *Always doing everything the same way.* Every group has a tendency to fall into a routine. Spontaneity helps keep people alert and learning. Mix things up; add variety; and allow others to participate in different ways.

Say: Now let's go through the first few minutes of a lesson. As we do, we'll discuss what works well for you and what does not.

Point out the teaching helps in the Leader's Guide introduction, then pass the book around so that your students can glance at the material. Using your Leader's Guide, have group members role-play the Sharing and Discussion times in Step 1. Ask students to take turns playing the leader. Then allow other group members to tell how they would handle the discussion differently.

If possible, you may want to take extra time to role-play an entire lesson. Give each group member a chance to assume the role of leader, asking other members to give positive critiques after each person has his turn.

Go over the Action Point at the end of the Study Guide.

Closing and Prayer (2–3 minutes)

Say: Since this is our last session, let us take a few moments to pray for each other and our new ministries. **With members sitting in a circle, begin by praying for the person on your left, then ask the next person to pray for the person on his left. After everyone has had a chance to pray, close by thanking God for the privilege of making disciples.**

Follow-Up

Encourage members to keep in contact and to help each other in ministry. Keep encouraging your disciples to build their discipleship ministries. Plan a fun time for the group members after a few weeks have passed.

Student Lesson Plan

Your Leadership Role

Following are the principles of good leadership:

1. *A good leader builds an atmosphere of trusting God* (John 14:1). Our Lord must be the focus of our study groups. We do not merely study about God, we get to know Him personally and learn to trust Him with every area of our life and ministry.

2. *A good leader encourages a mindset of ministering to others* (Romans 15:2; 1 John 3:17). We do not want to become ingrown (considering only our own interests), but rather reach out to others to meet their needs.

3. *A good leader cultivates an attitude of loving relationships* (John 13:34). Many factors can cause people to join a group, but only loving, Christ-centered relationships will keep them involved.

4. *A good leader creates a vision for reaching his community and the world* (Matthew 24:14). Acquiring a vision does not happen by itself; the leader must help the vision develop. Help students find a vision for helping to fulfill the Great Commission by praying together for your community and the world and by sharing witnessing experiences.

5. *A good leader provides loving accountability for group members* (Galatians 6:1,2). Greater spiritual growth results when Christians encourage each other to do the right thing. Here are ways you can help group members be accountable:

   a. *Get involved in their lives.* Do not just meet once a week, but get involved in the day-to-day lives of others and encourage them to do the same.

   b. *Help members apply God's holy Word to their lives.* Study the Bible with them, then model how to live the principles. Help them apply what they are learning to specific areas of their lives. Encourage them to set spiritual goals and pray with them about achieving these goals.

c. *Minister together.* Practical application is essential to learning. Imagine a doctor learning how to do surgery from a book! To help members, walk alongside them as they develop the necessary skills to witness, conduct follow-up appointments, and lead a group. Then hold them accountable for using their skills.

Leadership Questionnaire

Jot down a skeleton of your normal weekly schedule:
Sunday:
Monday:
Tuesday:
Wednesday:
Thursday:
Friday:
Saturday:

1. What activities can I eliminate as time wasters?
2. What blocks of time can I best use for ministry?
3. What blocks of time will I mark off for other responsibilities, such as family time, personal needs, or fun?
4. How can I change my discipleship ministry to help maximize my time for the Lord?

The Role of a Discipleship Group

A Plan to Evangelize

My plan for evangelism is:

An Environment for Growth

We must help our disciples become active members of the body of Christ, not just a part of our ministry group.

Read Romans 12:3–8 and 1 Corinthians 3:5–9 and answer these questions.

- What might happen if students are limited to one person's leadership for an extended period of time?
- What are some ways we are connected to other ministries?
- How can being a part of a church and of other ministries contribute to members' growth?

Discipleship is an exciting ministry for many reasons. Lively interaction with a variety of people and growing interpersonal relationships provide an enriching experience. These are the main elements of a healthy group environment.

1. *Sharing:* In your opinion, why is a sharing time important for connecting with each other?
2. *Prayer and praise time:* How has prayer helped you during our study times?
3. *Discussion:* In your opinion, what are the pitfalls of a discussion time? How can a leader help eliminate them?
4. *Building a vision:* How has your vision changed as a result of attending this group?
5. *Training:* How has this training helped you in your witnessing?
6. *One-on-one help:* What might happen to individual spiritual growth without one-on-one training outside of class time?
7. *Personal relationships:* What has been the most enjoyable for you during the weeks our group has met?

Selecting Disciples

It is important to look for the following qualities in the Christians we disciple. The person who is growing in these areas will likely become a good disciple-maker. For each person you plan to ask to join your new discipleship group, use the following list to evaluate his qualities as a potential disciple.

Qualities of a Potential Disciple

1. *A heart for God:* Does the person have a deep commitment to seek God? Here are some ways to tell:

   What does he talk about?

   Does his conversation tend to center around the Lord?

   Do his decisions glorify God?

2. *Dependence on the Holy Spirit:* Does the person demonstrate the fruit of the Spirit (Galatians 5:22,23) in daily life?

   Does he demonstrate faith in tough circumstances?

   How does he respond when things do not go well?

3. *Teachability:* Does this person ask questions about God's Word and ministry?

4. *Ability to build relationships:* Does the person have close friends?

   Do people like to be around him?

   Does he like to be around people?

   Does he give of himself to others?

5. *Relational thinking* (relating all areas of life to an ultimate purpose of glorifying God): Does this person have the purpose in life to glorify God?

   Does he relate decisions to this purpose and organize life's details around this purpose?

6. *Availability:* God is not looking for people with exceptional ability, but those who will be available for His work. Will this person make time for witnessing and being part of a Bible study? Does he follow through with his commitments or does he begin a task to abandon it when something more "exciting" comes along?

Steps to selecting disciples:

1. Ask God if He is leading you to work with this person.
2. Meet with this person individually and share your vision for fulfilling the biblical call to spiritual multiplication. Be specific about how God can use a small group in these ways:
   - To help him in his spiritual growth and ministry
   - To contribute to his fellowship and relationships
   - To provide personal training in how to share his faith
3. Explain what is required of a member in your discipleship group: to model godly living in your Christian life, a commitment of time, and witnessing as a lifestyle.
4. Give him a few days to think over his decision. Tell him that you will be praying for him, and that you will check with him on a certain date to find out his answer. Assure him that a "no" answer will not change your relationship.

Leading the First Meeting

The following practical tips will help you avoid some of the common pitfalls of leading a group.

- *Losing sight of your objective.* Remember that your objective is to build spiritual multipliers, not just lead a Bible study group.
- *Lack of ministry with group members.* Your group will not begin to multiply spiritually unless you and your students develop a lifestyle of evangelism, follow-up, and discipleship. Much of this must take place outside the group meetings.
- *Lack of prayer.* Only the Holy Spirit can enable you and your students to multiply spiritually. A lack of prayer indicates a lack of dependence on God. Schedule time for prayer, so you will not put it off.
- *Weak selection of group members.* The temptation a leader faces is to allow people to be part of your group who are not faithful, available, and teachable. It is much better to

train one person who goes on to train others than to have ten or fifteen people who never apply the principles.

- *Little personal involvement with members.* If you meet only during group time and an occasional ministry appointment, you will not be able to help them apply the principles of spiritual growth in their lifestyle. Plan social times too.
- *Leading a poor discussion time.* Leading a discussion is an art. As you become more experienced, you will find methods of discussion that fit your leadership style. Until then, remember these tips:

  Poor preparation can stifle discussion. Good preparation helps students get the greatest benefit from the lesson questions.

  Dominating leadership quenches discovery. Allowing everyone to share, ask questions, and express opinions or needs helps you better understand your group's strengths and weaknesses. It also makes members feel more valued.

  Asking ineffective questions, such as ones with yes and no answers, limits discussion. Good questions will help students think deeply and apply the principles to their lives.

  Little or no application will keep the discussion from becoming profitable. Pointing out the biblical principles and relating them to everyday life will help produce life changes.
- *Always doing everything the same way.* Every group has a tendency to fall into a routine. Spontaneity helps keep people alert and learning. Mix things up; add variety; and allow others to participate in different ways.

Action Point: Step 2 presented a chart called "Process for Building Multiplying Disciples." Refer to the chart as you prayerfully fill out each section of the following table. This table will help you plan your discipleship ministry in the weeks ahead.

Win	The people I have introduced to Christ are: The plans I have for witnessing in the next few weeks are:
Build	New Christian(s) I am following up are:
Train	New Christians or older Christians I can take with me witnessing are:
Send	Christians I believe would be interested in beginning a discipleship ministry are:
My Part	I feel God is leading me to participate in a discipleship ministry by:

BILL BRIGHT is founder and president of Campus Crusade for Christ International. Serving in 155 major countries representing 98 percent of the world's population, he and his dedicated team of more than 113,000 full-time staff, associate staff, and trained volunteers have introduced tens of millions of people to Jesus Christ, discipling millions to live Spirit-filled, fruitful lives of purpose and power for the glory of God.

Dr. Bright did graduate study at Princeton and Fuller Theological seminaries from 1946 to 1951. The recipient of many national and international awards, including five honorary doctorates, he is the author of numerous books and publications committed to helping fulfill the Great Commission. His special focus is *New**Life**2000*, an international effort to help reach more than six billion people with the gospel of our Lord Jesus Christ by the year 2000.

Response Form

☐ I have received Jesus Christ as my Savior and Lord as a result of reading this book.

☐ I am a new Christian and want to know Christ better and experience the abundant Christian life.

☐ I want to be one of the two million people who will join Dr. Bright in forty days of fasting and prayer for revival.

☐ Please send me **free** information on staff and ministry opportunities with Campus Crusade for Christ.

☐ Please send me **free** information about other books, booklets, audio cassettes, and videos by Bill Bright.

NAME____

ADDRESS____

CITY_____________________ STATE_____ ZIP__________

COUNTRY_______________________________________

Please check the appropriate box(es), clip, and mail this form in an envelope to:

Dr. Bill Bright
Campus Crusade for Christ
P.O. Box 593684
Orlando, FL 32859-3684

You may also fax your response to (407) 826-2149 or send E-mail to newlifepubs@ccci.org. Visit our Web site at www.newlifepubs.com.